THE YEAR A ROOF RAT ATE MY DISHWASHER

AN ARIZONA SURVIVAL GUIDE FOR ENTREPRENEURS

The Year A Roof Rat Ate My Dishwasher
An Arizona Survival Guide for Entrepreneurs

Copyright © 2018 by Denise P. Meridith

THE YEAR A ROOF RAT ATE MY DISHWASHER

AN ARIZONA SURVIVAL GUIDE FOR ENTREPRENEURS

DENISE P. MERIDITH

TESTIMONIALS

"I have known Denise Meridith since she arrived in Phoenix with the Bureau of Land Management, and subsequently managed her own public relations firm and non-profit youth sports organization. During the past 20+ years, I have admired her dedication to helping local governments, private businesses and non-profits enhance our quality of life here in Arizona."

-JERRY COLANGELO

PARTNER, JDM PARTNERS AND MANAGING DIRECTOR, USA MEN'S BASKETBALL

"Denise Meridith is a powerful, positive, engaging and inspiring individual! She is wealth of information and experience that literally encompasses the tools you need as an entrepreneur and business owner. Denise is truly the epitome of a natural leader as she engages every industry that it takes to build a thriving community in Arizona and national. Working with Denise is a must if you are looking to move to the next level."

-DR. VERNET A. JOSEPH

WORLD CIVILITY AMBASSADOR-NATIONAL STATESMEN SPEAKER-SERIAL ENTREPRENEUR-FOUNDER OF LIVE TO PRODUCE ENTERPRISES

"Women in Arizona are strong in small business. I cannot remember the statistics, but I believe that over 50% of businesses in Arizona are women-owned, most of these businesses qualify as small business. Small business will and is leading economic recovery in Arizona and this will continue. Women are at the forefront.

Denise is a great communicator and experienced professional, who demonstrates exceptional marketing and pubic relations skills. I know her to be a problem-solver, who successfully works through challenging and complex issues."

-BETSEY BAYLESS

FORMER ARIZONA SECRETARY OF STATE AND PRESIDENT EMERITUS AT MARICOPA INTEGRATED HEALTH SYSTEM

"Denise has been an important catalyst for the business community in her new adopted home of Phoenix. Through her outstanding networking skills and highly honed personal power of persuasion, she has been able to create partnerships, such as the Greater Phoenix Black Chamber of Commerce and the Arizona Tourism Alliance, which have empowered local businesses. She has been instrumental in attracting new businesses to the City and providing them the political and technical advice needed to ensure their sustainability. I would recommend her and her company, Denise Meridith Consultants Inc. to anyone wanting to get and stay connected in Phoenix."

-MICHAEL JOHNSON

FORMER MEMBER AND CURRENT CANDIDATE FOR PHOENIX CITY COUNCIL, DISTRICT 8

Denise is a master teacher and connector. If you are an Entrepreneur you need to read this book. Great job Denise, great book."

DR. WILL MORELAND
AMERICA'S #1 LEADERSHIP LIFE TRAINER

TABLE OF CONTENTS

PROLOGUE
THE YEAR A ROOF RAT ATE MY DISHWASHER

"Oh, sh—!" The repairman toppled backwards out from under the counter and landed on his backside on the kitchen tile floor.

"What is it?!!" I yelled, as I ran back into the kitchen. All I could think of was the time a plumber had a heart attack and died at my mother's house. Thoughts of 911 calls, a screeching ambulance, liability and insurance paperwork raced through my former-safety-officer-minded brain.

I got there in time to see him cautiously reach back under the counter, jiggle something and pull out a piece of PVC pipe that was gnawed through. "He ate right through the pipe!" he gasped, holding the half of a pipe aloof in wonder. "How big must he be?"

"Who's he?" I said nervously.

The plumber stood up unsteadily and starting to compose himself. That afternoon, he went on to explain how roof rats are attracted to sources of water. Evidently the pipe feeding my dishwasher was very attractive.

Ridding your life of a roof rat is no simple task in Phoenix, as I will explain later. I am not sure what ancestral indiscretion has unleashed roof rats, killer bees, Hanta virus-carrying mice, West

Nile-spreading mosquitoes, and other plagues upon the US' sixth largest city. While we have not experienced a zombie apocalypse yet, these are just some of the natural and unnatural disasters that have made life challenging for Arizona entrepreneurs the past 20 years.

But Arizona, also, has great weather, a low cost of living and easy access: qualities that make it an ideal place for ambitious and creative start-ups, a nurturing environment for entrepreneurs, like me. Since I am addicted to sunshine and allergic to snow, and, as I mentioned in my autobiography *Thoughts While Chillin'*, I have decided to stay in Phoenix forever, I have had to fortify myself against pestilence of the eight-, four- and two-legged kind. I will humorously share my lessons learned with others, who are already here or are thinking of coming here, in this Arizona survival guide for entrepreneurs.

CHAPTER 1
WHERE I LEFT OFF

The previous part of my autobiography *Thoughts While Chillin'* was published in the mid-2000's. Both Phoenix & I were doing great. People who know me, know I refer to the period of 2002-2009 as the time "when I was rich and famous." I used that book as a diving board for public speeches to government, private and non-profit workforces. I taught classes and started a weekly blog about leadership tips that is still growing, twelve years later. I shared my extensive experience as a consultant on a wide variety of projects and with clients from sole proprietors to famous people like Robert Kiyosaki or Donald Trump.

I love and have been involved in promoting NASCAR since 2002. But Phoenix, like a race car, took a curve too fast and hit a concrete embankment in 2009-2010. It took the worst hit of any major city in the US during the Great Recession. The roof rat incident I described in the prologue, and which inspired the title and cover of this book, was symbolic of that period from 2009-2013 in the 6th largest metropolis in America.

People who read Thoughts remember that I identified a favorite, happy, inspiring song every year. Well, my last favorite song was Eminem's Lose Yourself in 2002. Don't know whether it is due to the recession; the current, sorry state of music (most other baby boomers will agree with me on that); that MTV does not play music anymore; or that, since my career revolves around sports, the few times I still listen to the radio is to tune in to commiserate with my sports radio buddies, like John Gambadoro, Dave Burns and Ron Wolfley. So, sorry, there will not be old song lead-ins to the chapters this time.

Phoenix is back to setting the pace for job growth and housing sales. But many survivors of the recession are still worried, as their parents and grandparents, who survived the Great Depression, remained long after the event. With this sequel to part 1 of my autobiography, I want to share more lessons I have learned about entrepreneurship (vs the government career I discussed in Thoughts) and about how to survive-no, how to thrive from here on in Arizona.

CHAPTER 2
BEFORE TRUMP WAS TRUMP

Either people just have short memories, or this is evidence of the continuous turnover in Phoenix; but few people I have mentioned it to remember Arizona's encounter with the Donald. It was way back in 2004. Phoenix was growing, but still a small town. It has never been exposed to, or interested in, news beyond its borders, so we used to miss a lot of the crises, scandals and other to-dos that captivated Los Angeles or New York City. During most of my career in the West, I was busy managing millions of acres, hundreds of employees, worrying about cattle and copper, not what was happening in my home state. So, while I read and liked the advice in Art of the Deal and watched the first season of The Apprentice on TV, I had not heard about Donald Trump's role in the Central Park 5 or knew much else about the famous millionaire. Phoenix and I first encountered Donald Trump before he became Candidate Trump, POTUS, 45, or, in short, before Trump became Trump.

Phoenix had finally overcome its anti-Martin Luther King Holiday image and was becoming popular. Though the residential areas—Scottsdale, Chandler, Anthem--around the edges were growing, not much was happening downtown. Phoenix was one of the strangest big cities I had experienced. I had heard that there were once stores there, but shopping downtown Phoenix seemed like some urban myth when I got there in the late 1990's and Biltmore Shopping Square with Saks, Gucci and other upscale shops, five miles north of downtown, was the second most popular tourist attraction in the State. There was little public transportation to Washington or Jefferson Street and little reason for it unless you were working for the City or State, whose headquarters were there. People who came to visit me from out-of-town always thought Central Avenue near Indian School and Osborn was downtown, as that was where all but one (the tallest building in the State was the 38-story Bank One building near 1st Street and Van Bureau) of the big office buildings, full of executives and lawyers, were.

In 2004, Trump had a proposal to build a new hotel/residential complex on Camelback Road, across from Biltmore Square, which made sense. Biltmore had started to fade since an even fancier (and enclosed) mall-Scottsdale Fashion Fair—had opened up five miles to the east. This would have been a logical solution: more rich people moving into the area to live in the Trump complex, meant more shoppers for Biltmore, all contributing more tax dollars to Phoenix.

But, as I mentioned earlier, while being a great place to live and work, Mr. Spock would have been miserable here. Logic is not a strength of Arizona's.

Bayrock owned the land where the Trump development would go. I was friends with the Bayrock liaison. He was very excited, but was worried that there seemed to be growing opposition to the project, which would need the support of the Phoenix Council. Another consultant involved with the project suggested they hire me.

S.W.A.T. was a popular television movie in 2003. SWAT teams were highly skilled and trained police professionals, daredevils who are last-resort solutions to dangerous situations. While in BLM, I served a similar purpose, being transferred to reorganize offices, taking on problem employees others could not handle, evaluating and, if necessary, shutting down stalled programs. I continued to be a SWAT-like force as a consultant in Arizona, hired late in the process, to stop the bleeding, resuscitate the patient, avoid disaster.

Phoenix Councilman Claude Maddox, known for being direct, slightly profane and very entertaining, once summed it up to me: "How come everyone hires you after things are all f**ked up?"

If a damsel was dangling twenty feet above the ground, I was not going to risk my life climbing up to get her, but I would arrange for a net that would catch her and save her life. I enjoyed being a superhero, though being Black and a woman, I was seldom publicly recognized. But word-of-mouth kept me fully and happily employed.

But sometimes, they call you too late and the patient is too far gone to be resuscitated, or sometimes the damsel does not want to be rescued. A little bit of both was the case with the Trump project. The Trump organization had come to Phoenix with the same approach I am sure they had used successfully everywhere else: fancy brochures, promises of a shiny, new, ritzy Trump-branded building and Trump personally wooing the Mayor. But, as I always told my coastal clients, what works in New York, is almost guaranteed to fail in Phoenix.

First of all, Mayor Phil Gordon was determined to develop downtown Phoenix. He was particularly peeved about a pitiful, little rundown park area called Patriots Square Park right across from City Hall, where you did not want to be caught day or night. When there were no baseball or basketball games, there were no people. One New Year's Eve, I and a visiting friend did not see one other person when we walked about half a mile from a performance at Symphony Hall to Alice Cooper's Restaurant-- Cooperstown, the only place that was having any festivities.

"Is this safe?" she said nervously looking around as we walked down the dark, quiet, deserted blocks.

"Of course," I laughed. "There's no one down here to do anything to you."

Gordon was taking a hard line, pushing Trump about developing downtown instead. I doubt Trump was interested in taking the lead in rehabilitating the image of downtown Phoenix. The wealthy Biltmore area was more to his liking and image. I probably would have let Trump do his thing first in Biltmore, and then, if all went well, he could do future developments elsewhere in the metropolitan area.

Secondly, someone with Trump's image would have a hard time winning the hearts and minds of many Phoenicians. There was a lot of support for the project from business people and many others in the area. But there is an old adage about not trying to defeat a grandmother in tennis shoes. In this case, Trump was Goliath to David: a tiny, but very vocal group of residents, who doggedly attended Council and community meetings, effectively using the media. I would have recommended what I call the Disney approach. If Disney has an idea or proposal, they pursue it very quietly and discreetly. No hoopla, no Disney name tags, no offices opened up with Disney on the door. Until the final paperwork is signed, you did not even know it was Disney. They will be tough negotiators and stealthy networkers, seeking not to stir up, antagonize, turn off anybody, but get what they want. But it was impossible to undo the Trump first impression. My advice to any entrepreneur or business moving to Phoenix is that while Phoenix is a friendly town, it prefers quiet to proud and loud, even if loud is logical and successful.

Another lesson for entrepreneurs and for businesses is not to let anyone else define your image. You need to get out front and brand yourself. In this case, I would have avoided any use of the term "tower" in relation to this project. Trump Tower in New York City is 58-stories and 664-feet tall. The project opposition continually referred to "the Trump tower," leading people to envision something it was not. As I remember, the final plan for the Camelback building was about 14 stories. An animated graphic that I would have used, if I had had more time, showed the Trump complex being picked up, put inside Chase Field, and stadium roof closing over it. The Trump project in Phoenix would have been 200 ft; Chase Bank is almost 500 feet tall. Since that time, of course, there have been several buildings over 250 feet, which have been approved and constructed in Phoenix.

Ironically, Trump would later become an expert at defining images of others to their disadvantage. Opponents seemed to have no comeback for "Crooked Hillary," "Sloppy Steve," and "Little Marco."

Three months after I was hired, Trump got tired of waiting, abruptly shut down the effort, and, I heard a rumor that he signed a deal with Philadelphia soon after. Before leaving town, one of the Trump people said, "I wish we had hired you sooner." I did too. I would have welcomed the challenge, and made a lot more money, if I could have turned this around!

Downtown languished for years to come. A beautiful renovation of the Phoenix Convention Center was completed just in time for a combination of passage of State Bill 1070, a ridiculous anti-immigration piece of legislation that set off boycotts of Arizona like the MLK holiday issue had, and the recession, to flatline tourism. But another idea—Mayor Gordon and ASU President Michael Crow agreeing to move 2000 students from the College of Public Programs in Tempe to a new downtown campus in 2006—proved to finally spark downtown development. Along with University of Arizona and Northern Arizona University, a plethora of new programs, buildings and over 12,000 students have ultimately attracted housing, restaurants and entertainment to a now-thriving downtown.

Mayor Gordon also ultimately got to see another of his dreams come true. David Evans and Associates turned the squalid Patriots Square Park into part of a $900 million multi-block mixed-use development. Today CityScape is an attractive hub that includes a luxury hotel, restaurants, retail, residents and entertainment, where you can go to comedy shows, hear live music, and even go ice skating in the winter.

Donald Trump Jr. actually had the lead for the Phoenix project. He was very pleasant and expressed gratitude for our help. I never really had any conversations with him beyond small talk about the outdoors. It was obvious he did not have the temperament (or temper?) of Donald Sr., or the drive. Of course, in recent years, after reading about his volatile relationship with his father, I wonder if this project was one of his early attempts to win his father's attention and approval (he had joined the Trump Organization only a few years before) and how its failure affected their relationship.

Donald Trump Sr. sent me a signed copy of "The Way to the Top." I have previously told stories about my mother and me standing by stage doors on Broadway to get autographs when I was a kid. Though I have a lot of autographs, I have not been as crazy about them as I was when young. But I was excited this time: 1) because I was not getting much acknowledgement for my work (though I was gladly accepting big checks instead of thank yous or awards!), and 2) I thought it might be worth something someday. Trump was becoming quite a famous TV celebrity. I could never

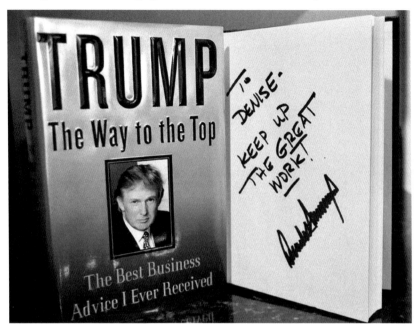

have imagined that it was the signature of someone who would make it to the top, who would become President of the US!

Real estate mogul Donald Trump Sr. sent me an autographed copy of Trump: The Way to the Top, thanking me for my work on his proposed development on Camelback Road near Biltmore Fashion Square, a project that did not work out for Phoenix in the early 2000's.

CHAPTER 3
WHEN I WAS RICH AND FAMOUS

Once in a while, I have an out-of-body experience where I see myself as the old medicine woman sitting on the rock, surrounded by the youth of the tribe, wide-eyed youngsters who love to hear my tales about an old life they cannot imagine. My stories about Phoenix before the recession might as well be about the color of dinosaurs. The kids are both curious and unbelieving as, like a DJ scratching records, I tell stories about what Phoenix was like in the 90's…when I was rich and famous.

Growing up in New York City in the '50's and early '60's, we did not know we were poor. Everyone in the Queens neighborhood was in the same straights. We all knew one or two men, who had "made it," in sports or maybe entertainment, who would come back to show us their new Cadillac or tell us about their apartment in Manhattan. They were not bragging; we enjoyed them coming to share their good fortunes. There was no Lives of the Rich and Famous on television then to continually show us what we were missing or should be craving.

My father, Glenarva Meridith, was in the service, so we had a regular paycheck. Everyone did. Everyone had a job, just not a high-paying one. My mother and I would take the $5 my Dad would send us from wherever he was stationed, and walk to the grocery store. Most necessities were in walking distance in NY. Within a few blocks, there were the butcher, bakery, candy store, hardware store, schools, five-and-ten cent store, laundromat, and movie theater. You could also walk a block or two to where the bus stopped, which would take you to the subway which transported you anywhere in the magic city from Broadway to Coney Island to the Polo Grounds. With the worn $5 bill we could fit four big brown paper bags of groceries from the A&P Supermarket into our metal shopping cart to wheel home.

Many fresh items were actually delivered to our house. We were visited weekly by the milk man, the bread man, and the soda man. Trucks came through with fresh fruit or fish. We kids enjoyed the adventure of going to the distribution centers to pick up the "government cheese," that was made available periodically. There was no crime. No one locked their door. No one had more than anyone else did; so what was there to steal? Plus everyone knew everyone else, including the cop that lived next door. Police were from the 'hood, too.

I felt blessed to have grown up in this environment. If you grow up poor, you are not surprised or discouraged when it happens to you again later in life. You know how to cope. But, I digress. Let's get back to the stories I tell youth about Phoenix in the '90's…back when I was rich and famous.

I arrived in Arizona in 1995. l moved to what was then "central Phoenix." I was five minutes from work, ten minutes north of downtown. The Biltmore area was the first area I saw when I was house-hunting and after looking at 19 other properties throughout Phoenix and the East Valley (remember as a native New Yorker, there was no way I was going to drive from the West Valley every day to work!), I returned to the wonderful 3-bedroom, 2-bath Santa Fe style home on 12th Street.

In fact, it and the backyard looked almost identical to the California house I had loved in the early '90's. Plus it had unique touches, like stained glass windows, a swing for two in the backyard, and a huge bird of paradise—a South African plant that may not bloom until its seventh year.

Phoenix was a small town. There was one of everything. The one Kinkos I went to (back when you had to go to the store to make color copies and send faxes) had a dirt parking lot that got muddy when it rained. People who were moving to Phoenix may not have been considered wealthy in outrageously expensive New York or California; but they seemed rich in Arizona, which had among the lowest wages and cost of living of any big city. I could have and considered buying two houses when I moved to Phoenix from Washington, DC. But instead I bought the 12th Street house, some vacant land and one of my best investments ever: one of the first Disney World timeshares.

Just as I felt comfortable and like everyone else in the neighborhood as a child, as an executive in government and private industry, in my network, we all felt we were in the same socio-economic boat—in this case, a very comfortable one, through the early 2000's. There was a growing, influential group of Hispanic-American businesspeople. Though a small percentage (5%) of the population, many African-Americans were either long-term, established community leaders or new executives and officials that arrived in corporations or government. Blacks were very influential then in Phoenix. They held high positions in corporations, the state legislature, the military and other Federal and local government agencies. While, there was still plenty of prejudice in Arizona, the Martin Luther King Holiday fiasco was in the past, and progress seemed to be getting made in an unusually bi-partisan state (which was almost evenly split between

Democrats and Republicans, and continually flipped back and forth between Democratic and Republican governors).

I was well-paid when I arrived as the Arizona State Director of the Bureau of Land Management (BLM). The positions and projects in which I was involved gave me a lot of connections and visibility. Accomplishments in which I was involved included designation of four BLM National Monuments and many other special wildlife and recreation areas; initiation of the legislation for designation of the Arizona Trail as a national scenic trail; passage of the legislation authorizing the new multi-purpose stadium for the Arizona Cardinals (now the State Farm Stadium) in Glendale; sale of the land to Tempe for creation of the Tempe Town Lake; reintroduction of endangered condors to Arizona; and the founding of the Greater Phoenix Black Chamber of Commerce and the Arizona Tourism Alliance. I was on many community boards and committees for non-profits. I had regular columns in the Arizona Republic and Phoenix Business Journal. I was loving Phoenix and it was loving me back.

When I retired early (very rarely, the Federal government provides an opportunity for employees to retire based on years of service rather than age), I slid easily into my new venture as CEO/President of my own public and community relations firm, that focused on hospitality. I originally had entitled it "Turbo Advertising." But a mentor of mine cautioned me that people wanted to hire me, not just any PR firm. So, in 2001, I excitedly incorporated Denise Meridith Consultants Inc (DMCI) as an S-Corp, headquartered in Phoenix!

I and my cohorts continued to prosper in the first half of the 2000's. I had never seen a better business environment in the US. Phoenix's low taxes and "y'all come" attitude made it an excellent place to start a business. The quality of life was incredible. Sunshine every day, warm winters, new housing, low crime, wonderful recreation (everyone then was golfing or playing tennis), and increasing cultural opportunities (e.g., symphony, ballet, theater, concerts, museums, etc.).

The corporations already in town were headed by progressive leaders, who were vested in the community. When I started the Black Chamber of Commerce, the CEOs did not send their HR or EEO people; they came themselves. Luckily for me, many other corporations from elsewhere were anxious to come to paradise then. As a Black female, while I was liked and respected, not many Arizonan white executives were interested in actually paying me. All of my clients came from Atlanta, New York and California, where more executives evidently both valued diversity and the importance of public relations. I was a great communicator due to my education and journalism experience; so, I served as, what I call, a "Phoenician translator."

Business is very different on the coasts. One of business mogul Donald Trump's most truthful sayings about New York City's attitudes was: "It's business, not personal." I have often tried to explain the NYC mindset to people in the West. New Yorkers (with their mixtures of Italian, Black, Greek and Jewish cultures) are very loud, emotional and outspoken about issues. They are well-read and educated and love to debate… everything. Two employees could be standing in the office yelling at each other about something the Mayor said, then suddenly stop and say "Hey, it's time for lunch. Do you want to go to Joe's Pizza? Great. Let's hurry to get a good table." Business and personal actions and attitudes can be separated. If two people can make a million dollars, they can put aside any personal differences. Also, they are very lineal and logical, i.e., A + B = C in NYC.

During my many years in the non-California West, I have found a very different attitude. Demeanor is critical, overriding. Loudness, assertiveness, sarcasm, profanity-all staples of leaders in New York and Washington, DC.—can be lethal in Arizona, Utah or New Mexico. People stab people in the back…but quietly. Also, most decisions in Arizona seem to be made on a personal basis. "I like you. We can make a deal," or "I don't like you. I do not care how much money we can make or good we can do. I'm not working with you." It is almost always whom you know, not necessarily what you know. Therefore, it is critical to know who the influencers are, and, in Phoenix, they are not necessarily the ones (e.g., a mayor or governor or CEO) that people from outside Arizona would expect. Having been an executive in government, business and non-profits, my network is unusually broad. My forte was (and continues to be) knowing whom to introduce to whom.

My MPA in organizational behavior from University in Southern California has been invaluable to my career re: this issue. Former Supreme Court Justice Sandra Day O'Connor is an advocate of everyone taking a course in public administration. I agree and recommend that every entrepreneur take at least one course in public administration. You would be surprised at what you learn about people as well as process, and how this knowledge can help you in business.

Since companies from the coasts are also willing to pay more for good service, I did very well recruiting companies and helping companies, trying to relocate, to do so with minimal hassle and expense. I have had wonderful local clients as well, ones willing to try new ideas and techniques to reach new audience. I worked with Robert Kiyosaki, soon after Rich Dad, Poor Dad was published, to help establish and promote his brand here in Arizona. I remember the discussion about what colors to use (everyone knows now:

purple won). I learned a lot from Kiyosaki and my other clients, as I was helping them market their brands.

Having had humble beginnings, I would never really be a very good rich person. When I was rich and famous in Phoenix, I had a country club membership, shopped at Nordstrom's and travelled a lot (mainly on businesses to conferences, nice conferences all over the US, as well as China, Mexico and Canada). I saved and invested a lot of my money. I had gold cards, premier memberships, elite this, supreme that. But I kept my little 12th Street house and my preference for keeping my Toyotas a long time.

Maybe, as most Black people do, I understood that what the majority gives you (money, notoriety, security, etc.), it can easily take away. Years ago, Chris Rock told a story about the difference between being wealthy and being rich, and why Black people will never be wealthy. "Shaq is rich," he said. "The white man who signs his check is wealthy." Forbes' recent billionaires' list of over 2000 people included only three Black Americans.

No matter how rich, how popular, or how respected you are, there are many white Americans who still just think of you as a n-word (just because you do not spell it out, does not negate its impact). At best, you may be considered an "exception." Eddie Murphy (sorry I reference a lot of comedians; but comedy clubs were a major part of my entertainment life in NY and DC) said one day, as he was walking down a street, a car full of white teenagers drove by screaming racial insults at him. Once they got close, they recognized him and actually stopped and started yelling "Eddie, Eddie, we love you, man!"

Murphy went on to explain that, as rich and famous as he was, he could guarantee that the white janitor in the building did not want to change places with him. Such is the fate of African-Americans. Despite the idea of "the great progress" and "racial equality" some white people are promoting to justify their opposition to affirmative action, college scholarships, etc., racism seems inherent in America.

Some whites may sit next to you at work every day. But they do not want to sit next to you in church, or for you to marry their children, or have you manage their money, or pay you the same amount they do a less-qualified white employee. Despite hundreds of years of co-habitation, many of these white people know nothing personal about Blacks. They do not ask. They do not learn. They do not care. As a result, as an African-American, you can do your best, but never ever take anything for granted or have unrealistic expectations of success and security. That is why I was disappointed, but not surprised at what happened in Arizona in 2009.

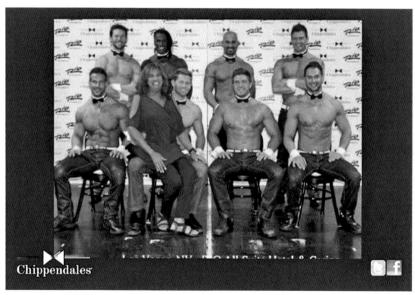

"Oh, those were the days." In this case it was the days when I was rich and famous. Regular trips to Vegas (to enjoy fun, decadent times like this one with the Chippendales) and international destinations, country clubs, season tickets and annual memberships to all the sports and cultural organizations, expensive art work, and traveling to give talks and autograph copies of my first book Thoughts While Chillin' were all benefits of my early retirement and successful public relations career before the recession.

CHAPTER 4
CRASH CART

For some reason, I love courtroom dramas on television, but hate medical dramas. As a kid, I liked Dr Kildare and Ben Casey because they were so good-looking. But, the last medical television show I liked was Quincy, M.E., because Jack Klugman acted more like a detective than a doctor. Maybe, it was those innumerable, repetitious scenes of the crash cart being rushed down the hall, people yelling "Clear," and dead people being jolted back to life.

I think back to 2009 as a scene from one of those medical shows. Phoenix had a sudden, unpredictable heart attack. People were running around frantically calling for the crash cart. But no amount of electric shocks could bring the body back to life and by the end of the year, we were all standing around clueless and in shock.

In 2000, Phoenix had a population of 1.3 million, up from the 1.13 million the five years before when I arrived. By 2009, the population had jumped to 1.6 million. I had always thought of Phoenix as a tourist destination. Tourism is the #1 export industry in Arizona. My goal as the Arizona State Director for the Bureau of Land Management was to boost the Arizona economy, as other traditional industries, such as cattle, cotton, and copper had started to fade. The designation of four national monuments, upgrading of campgrounds and RV parks, and other recreational and cultural activities contributed to Arizona's attraction for domestic and international tourists.

But after 2000, more tourists and conventioneers were returning to stay, and then encouraging relatives and friends to move here. As prices in California and Illinois rose, the number of their residents moving to Arizona boomed. The sprawl was like kudzu (I will talk about that plant later), with communities springing up in areas farther and farther from the city of Phoenix, like Maricopa and Apache Junction. Spacious, new houses on bigger lots at lower prices were hard to resist. Canadians were also buying up properties as investments and Mexicans were immigrating in larger numbers.

I knew who the tourists were and why they were here. But the question I had re: the migration after 2003 was "Who are these people and where are they working?"

Having done a lot of work in economic development, I knew that, while corporations were making huge profits, they seemed to be downsizing, and there were not many major employers in the State. While tourism was a major employer, the wages were low and could be easily disrupted by unanticipated events, such as 9/11. Much of the growth in employment seemed to be related to real estate, e.g., realtors, mortgage lenders, construction jobs.

The other new phenomenon was that everyone became interested in the business of real estate. Teachers, lawyers, nurses, all types of professionals were taking the real estate exams, enrolling in house-flipping courses, buying multi-family units, building houses for family members next to theirs. I am reminded of the 2015 award-winning film—*The Big Short*—about the stock market collapse, in which the pole dancer talked nonchalantly about owning five houses and a condo. Phoenix has a sordid history in real estate scams; but it appeared we were all involved in this get-rich-quick scheme.

I will not go into detail about the financial bust; plenty has been written about that. I will just talk about the impact on me and Phoenix. The crash happened even faster than the boom.

My business had flourished because of all those businesses wanting to move to or have conferences in Phoenix and needing an Arizona whisperer. I had government-related contracts because Phoenix was expanding facilities, from Convention Center to the Airport, to accommodate a growing hospitality trade. Like everyone else, I also had acquired rapidly-appreciating multi-family facilities. When the crash hit, small businesses died, unemployment soared, corporations stopped plans to come in 2009. The passage of State Bill 1070, a rabidly anti-immigrant law, killed what little tourism was left, leading to a boycott and ultimate loss of $90 million in conventions in Phoenix. My government contracts were cancelled, conferences were rescheduled elsewhere, credit cards canceled all my credit, my rental property defaulted, and my income dived $150,000 within a few months.

I was luckier than most. The Federal pension covered the mortgage and provided healthcare. The old adage "Those who can do, those who can't teach" was never truer. I started teaching communications for Cornell University online. Gone were the country club, the Suns season tickets, the ballet and symphony performances, the cruises, Nordstrom's, expensive dinners (though the upscale restaurants disappeared too), the rental property. I had been in the process of selling my Lake Havasu property to pay down the house mortgage; but the sale closing date was delayed, and the property's sale wound up getting seized by the court instead. Even my monthly column in the *Phoenix*

Business Journal disappeared, as newspapers lost readership and tried to replace commentary on what was happening with paid advertisements.

As only having one sister—Rosa—who was 10 years older than me, I had spent most of my life entertaining myself. So, reading and writing (e.g., I continued my weekly blog on leadership) kept me occupied.

One of the things I chose to do was document this nationwide tragedy both in my memory and on paper. I went to job fairs and sadly watched highly-educated, former executives in their suits humbly handing their resumes to young people, who did not care, at exhibits for fast food restaurants and low-end rental cars. I saw formerly-hyped expensive housing developments with just a few houses on each block occupied, like ghost towns.

When I moved to Arizona, Phoenix Metro-Center had been one of people's favorite shopping centers. Dillard's, Macy's, Sears, all the big department stores were there, before the term one-stop-shopping was popular. But stores closed and the surrounding area deteriorated during the recession. Two times I went there, I witnessed police chasing suspected shoplifters down the halls. By 2010, it had gone into receivership. One day I walked in and the corridor was literally deserted; I did not see one shopper in either direction. As a movie buff, all I could think of was George Romero's *Dawn of the Dead*. I thought of zombies suddenly coming down the hall, chasing me. I was scared and left right away. It was symptomatic about how bizarre the whole city and situation had become.

I wrote stories about hardworking Phoenix residents who had lived in their neighborhoods for years, and due to losing jobs and/or health insurance, were forced into foreclosure. Meanwhile Wall Street moguls were bailed out. It was maddening. It seemed so unfair.

That's when I became determined to be what I have been since then: a good news reporter. I got a position as the Phoenix business reporter for *Examiner.com* with two online columns a week and minimal pay. But it became very fulfilling. I wrote inspirational stories about small, women-owned or minority-owned businesses that were surviving. I spread their lessons, examples and advice to an audience hungry for hope. I ultimately had the position with *Examiner.com* for seven years and wrote hundreds of articles, before itself went out of business. I hoped I helped both a lot of previously unrecognized businesses and underserved readers.

As I mentioned earlier, it is easier to adjust if you know that "wealth" is fleeting for people of color. "Last hired, first fired," occupational segregation and every other excuse created throughout history to displace people of color, was used to drive their unemployment to twice that of whites. I had plenty of company—of all colors—in bankruptcy. There was no shame unless you decided to take it on yourself. In fact, it became an advantage for everyone to file bankruptcy at the same time. The courts were so overrun, hearings were held in mass, paperwork was rubberstamped, and many people probably got away with little change of status, which might not have happened with more scrutiny. A friend of mine, who filed, years later, when the rush was over, was constantly hassled by creditors, courts, etc.

There was a kid's TV show called *Romper Room* that I used to watch. I have always been what was called a "do bee" on the show: a good little girl. So, I took the training, filled out all the monthly reports and probably wound up paying back more than I needed to through the years. At first there were long lines, waiting each month, at the courthouse to submit the monthly bankruptcy progress report. But, eventually, it looked like I was the only one tramping down there each month.

In early January 2013, my phone rang. It was a realtor that wanted some public relations assistance. Then there was another and another. The real estate professionals were the first professionals back and they wound up taking me with them. I did everything from help one to make donations to schools to being editor of *Home and Lifestyle Magazine*, a luxury real estate magazine.

It was a very slow recovery (Las Vegas and Phoenix were the hardest hit cities in the country). But as people in other parts of the country recovered, they started to flock to the still dirt-cheap houses available in Phoenix. Phoenix maintained its unique and attractive combination of great weather and professional sports venues, which draws large, profitable events like the Super Bowl, NCAA Final Four, World Baseball Classic, and bi-annual NASCAR weekends. The metropolitan area is being pumped up by the enthusiasm and progress of the smaller cities. Buckeye, Goodyear, Gilbert are among the fastest growing areas in the country. Tolleson, a town of only 6600, was voted the best place to start a business in Arizona by NerdWallet. As the memories of SB 1070 faded and universities, like ASU and GCU, bloomed, companies like Amazon and Apple, began to consider Phoenix competitive for expanding operations.

Journalism never recovered, though. I am continuing to seek out new ways to share lessons I and others have learned with entrepreneurs. I have maintained a weekly blog for years. Another way is teaching a live tourism, recreation and sports marketing course at ASU. I hope I am inspiring a new group of Gen Z'ers there to take Phoenix to even higher levels after graduation.

CHAPTER 5
DAMN TREES

*D*amn trees. That might seem like strange terminology to be used by a former environmental specialist. After all, trees were a positive influence in my childhood. Sturdy oaks were there for climbing and being sites for our tree houses, and maples provided shade for our backyard picnics. Spectacular elms lined the walkways to the Ag Quad at Cornell during my freshman year (though they were being killed off by senior year by Dutch elm disease). We thanked the Japanese for their gifts of the cherry blossoms every spring. Every fall, trees all awed us with a plethora of red, orange and yellow hues. People travel from all over the world to see these wonderful trees in the US.

But, according to Ecclesiastes 3, "To every thing there is a season, and a time to every purpose under the heaven." In Phoenix, the purpose of trees must be…to tease us and make us look foolish.

Though, growing up in New York City, we had an inherent hate of Californians, we secretly envied them. We dissed everything from their casual dress to their annoying Valley accents and their lack of sensible public transportation. New Yorkers never forget or forgive, so there are still folks ranting about the Dodgers' betrayal in 1950. But one of my fantasies was to retire in a place with palm trees, those tall, majestic symbols of ideally warm weather with their fronds swaying gently in the breeze. So, when the realtor pulled into my HOA of streets lined with palm and grapefruit trees (another NYC fantasy: to be able to go outside and pick a fresh grapefruit or orange off your tree for your morning breakfast!), I knew I had reached the promised land.

What better omen than to buy a house on Palo Verde Drive? I had seen pictures of palo verde trees and loved their unique green trunks. But my first clue that something was amiss should have been that there were no Palo Verde trees on Palo Verde Drive. In fact, I was soon advised never to consider planting one.

Being a wildlife biologist, and while I had the best flower garden in the block in DC where I had moved from, I never paid that much attention to trees, except to photograph the cherry trees in the spring and the colorful aspens and maples in the fall. But it seemed I had hit pay dirt with the nice variety at my new Arizona home.

There was a beautiful oak shading the southeast corner of the yard. Two palm trees towered at the front entrance. A spectacular weeping willow graced the side patio and looked great from the street. Then there was a mulberry tree, liked the one I grew up with, and a couple of wonderful, bountiful grapefruit trees. All of them would individually and eventually haunt me.

The HOA had been built on an old orchard; ergo all the grapefruit and orange trees. They were beautiful and fruitful. In DC, you had to worry about leaves clogging your rain gutters. In Phoenix, it was the grapefruits themselves that required you climbing a ladder to drag them out of gutters. The other thing I learned is that, while beautiful, grapefruit trees are short-lived. The recession of the 2000's was made even more depressing by the decade-long die-off of our beloved grapefruit trees. By 2011, my beloved grapefruit trees were gone.

The weeping willow had to be removed as its spectacular sheath of leaves started to obstruct the sidewalk and public signage and the trunk strained against the HOA boundary wall.

There are a wide variety of palms (fan, queen, date, etc.) throughout Phoenix, none of which apparently, to the surprise of most people, are native plants. Yes, palms are drought resistant. But palm trees need to fed and fertilized. They require annual trimming and treatment for an assortment of bacteria, bugs and viruses. They grow rapidly upward, providing no shade. Falling fronds dirty ponds and coconuts can clobber cars. Having a palm tree is like having pet that does not provide you any unconditional love.

The most startling tree encounter was with the oak tree. One day, I brushed next to a branch and a few leaves fell off. I was surprised as it was not autumn; these leaves were not red or orange, nor did they have any insects or apparent fungus on them. Here was a large, healthy looking tree, full of shiny green leaves, but if you touched one of the leaves, it would just drop off! The tree was dead, but still standing.

My guess is that it was a fungus, deep in the soil, that can affect trees summers after they are planted, when their roots reach the affected areas. It may take years for trees to show symptoms and the tree can die within a few days of the first symptoms. The leaves stay attached to the affected plant. More money had to be spent to have the tree carted off. People recommended immune or heartier trees that could be planted instead were palo verdes and palm trees! No thanks!

In the 1970's, the HOA was built on an orchard and 12th Street used to be lined with grapefruit trees. I discovered that grapefruit trees have short lives (about 30 years) compared to many other trees. This straggler is the lone survivor in 2018.

CHAPTER 6
BABOONS AND OTHER NATURAL DISASTERS

For many years, while living in Phoenix, I experienced dust storms. A warning signal would interrupt the DBacks game on radio, and, later technology would send loud screeches through our cell phones, which would give us plenty of warning. Like a dense fog, dust would preclude visibility for 30 minutes or so. Of course, the same fools that would try to drive through blizzards in Pennsylvania or outrun forest fires in California, would stay on the freeway, run off the road or crash into each other. But Phoenicians would say we love living in Arizona because there are no natural disasters, real ones that is.

All of us immigrants had survived and escaped the earthquakes, tornados, floods, blizzards, mudslides or other forces of nature that brought death and destruction. Dust storms...eh? But, evidently, meteorologists or media or both, were bored, or envious of their coastal brothers and sisters on television, drenched and hugging railings during storms to demonstrate what 60 mph gusts meant. There is an Arabic word "habb," which means to blow, and haboobs described sandstorms in the Sudan. So suddenly, a few years ago, weather people in Phoenix were gleefully talking about "haboobs."

The videos look very spooky and dramatic on television…a gigantic wall of dust slowly engulfing downtown Phoenix. But it reminds me of one of my favorite old horror movies. Remember a teenaged Steve McQueen trying to outrun a huge blob that was running over the buildings in his small town? Except in real life, the haboob is less threatening, even as it passes through town. In fact, an acquaintance of mine (and excellent sports reporter) Pedro Gomez from ESPN will forever hear about the end of the autocorrection to his July 30 tweet:

"@Rangers (https://twitter.com/Rangers) and @Dbacks (https://twitter.com/Dbacks) delayed in downtown Phoenix because a baboon went through town and overloaded the grid, knocking some lights out."

I found it funny, but very understandable, since most people can't remember or spell the word anyway.

This is not to say that Phoenix is without its freak incidents. Once in a while, a "microburst" will take out a few blocks in a pattern and a way that looks suspiciously like a tornado. For some reason, microbursts seem to only like Glendale, Arizona. Then some people may drown in flash floods, camping in or driving though washes. Others fall off or have heat strokes hiking in local peaks.

But the lack of natural threats is a great asset, not only for your health, but your business. There are no snow or hurricane days to disrupt workforce attendance. As a manufacturer, you can ship easily year-round. Company picnics are generally rain-free. You do not have to hire snow-removal companies to shovel heat.

CHAPTER 7

CLOVER BURRS, KUDZU AND OTHER SCIENCE *NON*-FICTION HORRORS

When I was a young professional in BLM, working in the Southeast, the kudzu crisis hit the US. It is a vine in a group of plants in the pea family "*Fabaceae*." It was introduced to the US by Japan in the late 1800's. Kudzu was originally looked upon favorably as a source of shade, a good food for livestock, an herbal medicine, and a mitigation for soil erosion. The government actually paid people to plant it. By the 1970's when I arrived in BLM, it had become a noxious weed, covering over seven million acres. Again, like *The Blob*, time-lapse photography shows it growing unbelievably fast, choking out other plants, uprooting trees, covering cars and sheds. As if that was not enough, it, like cockroaches, was hard to kill. It could survive droughts, frosts, nitrogen-poor soils, and was becoming resistant to herbicides.

It was a scary time. But like mad cow disease, Ebola, flesh-eating bacteria and many other sci-fi-type crises, and though it still causes hundreds of millions in lost forest productivity, we have survived. Why I bring this up is that what happened to me in

Phoenix in the summer of 2018 gave me flashbacks to the horrors of kudzu.

Of course, I would love to have a beautiful, jade-green Kentucky blue grass-covered lawn like people have back in DC, but in the desert, for over 20 years, I have been content with barely ground-covering Bermuda grass in the backyard for the dogs. In the spring of 2018, I noticed the usual dandelions and some scattered clusters of clover. Within two months, the lawn looked like a wheat field after the harvest, littered with tangles of an ugly vine-type weed. I used the *Naturalist* app (one of the most useful apps I have) to identify the culprit: burr clover (*Medicago polymorpha*). What turned out to be the fruit of the plant were burrs covered with tiny hooks. Though it is a worldwide scourge, I had never encountered it before.

It quickly made the backyard unusable. I imagined burrs hopping onto me whenever I stepped outside. One day I picked 40 burrs from my poodle's curly coat. When I put the dog's mat in the washing machine, I wound up with burrs in my lingerie. When I sent a photo of my puppy to a friend, he asked where the photo was taken; my backyard was that unrecognizable.

I put on my biologist hat and started doing research via the Internet. I had to find something powerful enough to kill the clover, but not kill the grass or affect pets. I first tried weed killer granules; no success. Then on *Amazon.com* I found a listing for *Weed Beater Ultra*, a concentrate that was supposed to kill over 200 weeds (wow, maybe I can get rid of the dandelions at the same time) in 24 hours. I was as excited and nervous as Ralphie in one of my favorite movies—*A Christmas Story*—waiting for his mail order decoder pin.

I eagerly mixed my weed killer potion in an old-fashioned pump and charged around the yard. I did not believe the 24-hour pledge, but even if it took a week, I would be happy. I know it sounds strange to hear a biologist say it, but I was thrilled with the death and destruction I saw all over my yard the next day. All the clover and dandelions were brown and gnarled, while the grass, free at last, peeking through was bright green.

Before I arrived in Phoenix, I was forewarned by friends about other threats, not the usual big-city ones, like meth labs next door blowing up, or geologic ones like tsunamis. There are little ones, uniquely southwest, that may not impact your business, but can affect your personal bottom-line. I will pass these tips along, which I hope will enhance your overall quality of life in Phoenix.

Along with palm trees, another fantasy of New Yorkers was having your own swimming pool. When I was growing up in NYC, our swimming pool was a big corrugated metal thing you filled up with water from the hose every summer. In California and DC, I had hot tubs, which are wonderful, but did not seem practical in a place where summer temperatures reached 115 degrees. While everyone seemed to have a pool, a couple of friends warned against it. Unless you have young kids, who will use it daily for the next 15 years, having a pool is like having, umm…a palm tree.

With the heat, jumping into your pool in summer in Phoenix, is not the refreshing dip you get in California. Plus, the maintenance (algae, scorpions, palm fronds, pH levels) is either a full-time job or a major monthly expense. I had a friend that actually moved because of the burden of paying for a pool. During the 20+ years I have been in Phoenix, only three times have I ever thought "Gee, I would like to swim in a pool today." Therefore, I have not missed not having one.

Speaking of heat, everyone has heard the punchline "But it's a dry heat," but few people understand what that means. It means I have literally seen a gage register 0% humidity. As long as you are not jogging, 95 degrees feels great. I laugh at people from New Orleans, who are afraid to come to Phoenix in the summer because they are afraid it will be too hot. When I lived in Washington, DC, people kept a change of clothes in the office because your chance of getting from home to work on the Metro in the summer without being sopping wet was nil.

The average annual temperature in Phoenix is 75 degrees. After growing up in blizzards, ear muffs and mittens in New York, I have been more than willing to trade four months of 100 degrees for eight months of heavenly 77. Plus, if you are in tough business negotiations in Phoenix, your opposition never has to see you sweat.

Another warning I would give, that I did not know about before I bought my house, is to visit it in the rain. Of course, that is very difficult to do in a city with 350+ days of sunshine. But you can do some research on your potential home or business site before you buy it. Few people think of water being an issue in the desert. But Phoenix does not have a lot of those drainage grates. Good news is that kids do not have to worry about being eaten by Stephen King's *It*. Bad news is that there is no place for water to go. My house, just by luck, not design, is on the high ground of a cul-de-sac. But be sure your potential house or business is not in a floodplain or in any other vulnerable location.

I know I am a weird wildlife biologist. I love everything from insects to whales. I just do not want to co-inhabit the same space. If I want to see creatures. I want to venture into their environment or a zoo. I do not want them visiting me. Think about how much you love interacting with your fellow living beasts before you decide where to live in the Phoenix Metropolitan area.

I live in central Phoenix, 10 minutes from downtown. The roof rats seem to have been an anomaly; I have not seen one since that one exciting year of the dishwasher incident. This year is the first year, though, I have encountered mosquitoes. They are not the big B-52 types you see in the South; they are tiny. But they still bite! If you have dogs or cats, you need to regularly spray the lawn for ticks. Otherwise, I enjoy watching the hummingbirds and the butterflies that like the lantana flowers, and the occasional mockingbird that likes to tease my poodle.

The further away you move from downtown, the more exciting your adventure will become. On the larger side, there are the coyotes, bobcats, and someone told me about raccoons last week! They are all definite hazards for dogs and cats. On the smaller, creepier and more hazardous-to-people side are rattlesnakes, scorpions and tarantulas. All of these issues are controllable and, compared to mountain lions or bears in other areas of the state, are no big deal, just an added expense.

Other unanticipated personal or business auto expenses in Phoenix include car registration (Arizona has a value-based system, so vehicle that would cost me $65/year in New Mexico is over $400 on Arizona); tires and batteries (neither of which hold up well in 110 degree heat); and windshields (everyone has insurance for this, as rocks on I-10 can do you in every 18 months). While public transportation has improved somewhat during the past decade (e.g., the light rail service began in 2008), a vehicle is still a requirement in Phoenix. Budget accordingly.

Do the advantages of owning a house or business in Phoenix outweigh the disadvantages? You bet!

Wait! But what about those images of images of Hispanics being rounded up, militia men with upside down American flags, and the thought that you can take your Glock to dinner in Phoenix? Isn't Arizona the state that does not recognize the Martin Luther King holiday? Who would want to move to a place like that?

Three-month-old Arry Potta looks sad, sitting on my lawn, which was suddenly strangled by clover burrs. One night I had to pick 40 burrs out of his coat!

CHAPTER 8

SCOUNDRELS AND SCANDALS

Many American cities have had famous scandals throughout history. Some, like Chicago or New Orleans, have colorful histories and reputations. Before I moved to Phoenix, I had spent a lot of my life in Silver Spring, Maryland, still one of my favorite places on earth, and the Maryland/DC/Northern Virginia area certainly had some notable characters. As Governor of Maryland and, later, as Vice President, Spiro Agnew was investigated for taking kickbacks from contractors, conspiracy, bribery, extortion and tax fraud. Then there was the infamous Mayor Marion Barry, who, caught on video smoking crack, served jail time and four terms in office. One of his most famous quotes after being arrested in 1990 was "Goddamn setup...bitch set me up." I was reminded of this last August when I heard California Congressman Duncan Hunter blame his wife for misuse of campaign funds. Some politicians' denials of guilt and attitudes about women have not changed.

One of the most serious crises I lived through, which was a precursor to a Phoenix scandal and of which I was reminded during the Phoenix recession, occurred in 1985.

In an era of no PCs, cellphones, emails or texts to worry about, as I did every day, I got home from the BLM office in Silver Spring, flopped onto the coach and turned on the local television news. I still remember the pained look on the news anchor's face that day in May 1985 when he said, "The banks in Maryland are now closed."

Just as today, there seemed to be a bank on every corner of the city then. Friendly bank tellers you got to know and like, easy loans and transactions were the rule. Except what the general public did not understand was that their favorite banks did not have that little blue and white logo in the corner meant something. These Savings & Loans (S&Ls) were not like traditional banks; they were not Federally insured by FDIC.

Most people remember the scenes in everyone's favorite Christmas movie *It's a Wonderful Life,* where concerned depositors crowded into the bank, confronting George Bailey after Uncle Billy had lost the bank's $8,000. Well, Jeffrey Levitt looked a little like Uncle Billy, a malicious version. A convicted slum lord, he and his wife were arrested for stealing $14.6 million from his own Old Court Savings and Loan, which set off the run on the S&Ls and their collapse in Maryland, when there was no money to cover withdrawals. Greed fed by lack of regulation and oversight (which continues today) robbed residents of $9 billion.

It is still painful to recall the real-life suffering Companies had no money to pay employees. Employees had no money to buy groceries. Hand-drawn signs "NO CHECKS" went up in supermarkets and barbershops. Even if you had written a check the week before and it had not cleared, it meant you were in arrears on your mortgage or your electric bill or your child care.

I was luckier than most. There is a large population of Federal employees in the Maryland suburbs. The Federal government immediately froze paychecks that were scheduled to be directly deposited into S&Ls and gave payment directly to employees. Federal credit unions were able to process transactions. The S&L, in which I had an account (which ironically was named something like Government Savings & Loan), had filed an application for FDIC insurance before the closures. So, a month later, its application was approved, and all its depositors' money was covered and accessible. But most of the S&Ls were not in that position. Levitt went to prison…for a short while; he later opened a successful cigar business. Retirees lost their pensions and life savings permanently.

So, I have not been surprised by the scandals that have plagued Phoenix the past 20 years. But I am sometimes surprised by their congeniality or originality, and Arizona's ability to forgive, forget or overlook?

Phoenix sometimes seems to be on a time delay. It adopted Jim Crow laws long after they were installed in the South. Today, news stories that were in NYC newspapers may be reprinted in Arizona a week later. Likewise, though there had been the S&L failures in Ohio and Maryland in the mid-1980s, the political scandal did not hit Phoenix until 1989, when the Keating Five were accused.

A bi-partisan group of five US Senators—Alan Cranston, Dennis DeConcini, John Glenn, John McCain and Donald Riegle—allegedly persuaded the Federal Home Loan Bank Board to not take action against campaign contributor Charles Keating Jr, whose Lincoln S&L collapsed in 1989. Over 20,000 bondholders and investors were impacted, and the crisis cost the taxpayers $3.4 billion.

I will not waste much ink on most of the routine political scandals. Like Maryland, Phoenix has had problems with

Governors. Ed Mecham was known for his racist remarks and actions but got impeached for misusing public money in 1988. About 10 years later, Governor Fife Symington (who, ironically, is a Maryland native) resigned after being convicted for bank fraud. He was later pardoned.

Likewise, as most cities, Phoenix has continuing problems with sexually-abusive Catholic priests. Bishop Thomas O'Brien from the Catholic Diocese of Phoenix was embroiled in controversies about engaging in and ignoring sexual abuse of youth, committing a hit-and-run fatality, and other convictions and settlements until his death in 2018.

Another disheartening scandal that is still having negative impact and is still being mentioned in current political campaign ads is the Phoenix Veterans Administration (VA) Hospital. An estimated 40 veterans died waiting for care at the hospital and staff was accused of falsifying the data by a whistleblower in 2012. Problems remain as there has been a revolving door of seven directors between 2014 and 2017.

I would like to focus on the scandalous behavior which most challenges entrepreneurs in Arizona. What is most interesting to me is that Arizona has what I call "smiling scoundrels." They are not the stereotypical growling crooks in leather jackets or trench coats (too hot here for that) and dark glasses. They are well-dressed, well-educated, articulate, normal guys with families; they live next door, work out at your gym, go to your church. In other cities, like NY, Chicago or Detroit, there are serious consequences for screwing people. One may wind up at the bottom of the nearest body of water or not survive a prison sentence. Here, crooks seem to get away with misdeeds, and, often, are inexplicably forgiven, and allowed to repeat their deceptions over and over.

Sometimes, though making a killing is the ulterior motive, the scams start out or sound well-meaning. At a time in 2000, when Arizona was suffering from horrible air pollution, Arizona House Speaker Jeff Groscost pushed through a law that would provide state-funded rebates to people who bought cars and installed a second tank that burned cleaner fuel. Of course, nothing in Arizona is as simple as it seems or should be. By the end of this debacle:

◊ The state had only put aside $10 million for the program;

◊ Groscost removed the "new vehicle" language, that would have limited the number of eligible vehicles to 2700, thus making 35,000 vehicles eligible;

◊ The promised rebates were ridiculous tax credits that were 30-50% of the cost; the more you spent on the car, the bigger the rebate;

◊ The requirement was to install the alt-fuel tank, not use it;

◊ It was alleged a friend of the House Speaker was the only businessperson installing the tanks;

◊ There were rumors that the Speaker also made sure his ward parishioners knew about the program first;

◊ Once the word about the program got out beyond Mesa, the Governor did not sign legislation to stop things for two weeks, allowing the applications to grow from around 300 to over 3900;

◊ Those who had not applied before the State stopped the program had to haggle with dealers over any refunds.

◊ The State faced an estimated bill of almost $500 million, a third of the state budget, that was ultimately reduced to $200 million

◊ There was a big backlash against drivers of alt-fuel cars, which had special license plates, whether they participated in the program or not.

I remember everyone at work and home talking about the rebates that month. People were buying two cars. Businesses bought fleets. A friend of mine bragged to me about his brand-new Honda that would cost him only $6000 after the rebates. Everyone—politicians, people who bought the cars, people who missed out on buying new cars, environmentalists, dealers—was angry. Arizona was being ridiculed nationwide.

Groscost was voted out of office, which was not too much punishment for almost bankrupting an entire state. He might have ended up inside a car trunk in less-forgiving city. A few years later, Groscost was hired president of an alternative fuels company before he succumbed to a heart attack.

There have been many other questionable characters in real estate, business development, technology, government contractors—who live peaceably in Phoenix, continually coming up with new schemes and finding new victims. I have met quite a few of them and, also, encountered many people who are just uneducated, not intelligent or have no common sense (a friend of mine always said "Common sense ain't that common anymore"), who can lose themselves and you a lot of money. But the bulk of Phoenician businesspeople are polite, friendly, and aim to please. Guess 350 days of sunshine help keep people in a good mood.

My advice to entrepreneurs is simple common sense: if you do not know the person, vet them (e.g., Better Business Bureau, background checks) and ask a lot of other people who have been in town a long time about them. They may already be infamous. In Phoenix, if the deal sounds too good to be true, it is!

CHAPTER 9
THE WHITEST STATE IN AMERICA

A few years ago, when I was travelling often throughout the US, I actually hesitated to admit I was from Arizona. People, especially minorities, in other states, would look at me with a "I thought you were smart. Why would you live in Arizona?" glare. People thought I had chosen to live in a "racist state." There are some persistent myths about the State, but most of these feelings are based on what has happened throughout history in Arizona, and how it still often appears in the media today.

Arizona adopted Jim Crow laws later than some states (interracial marriage was banned in 1912 when Arizona became a state), but Phoenix did so with equal vengeance. Like the South, housing was segregated; people of color were not allowed to live north of Van Buren Avenue in Phoenix. The Paul Laurence Dunbar Elementary School and the Phoenix Union Colored High School (now the George Washington Carver Museum) were the "colored schools" in Phoenix. The bus or train station restaurants were the only places for Blacks to eat. The Black Philanthropy Initiative recently had a ceremony commemorating The Alston House—home and medical office of Dr. Lucius Alston who was the only doctor ministering to Blacks, Native Americans and Latinos in Mesa in the first half of the 20th century. African-Americans were discriminated against in employment, housing, voting, healthcare and education.

Lincoln Ragsdale, who founded the Greater Phoenix Council for Civic Unity, described it this way: "Phoenix was just like Mississippi. People were just as bigoted. They had segregation. They had signs in many places 'Mexicans and Negroes not welcome.'"

In 1986, Governor Bruce Babbitt had embraced the Martin Luther King Holiday as the rest of the nation had when President Ronald Reagan established it by declaration. Continuing racism against Blacks in Arizona was first highlighted nationwide, when his successor Evan Mecham rescinded the holiday as one of his first acts. Mecham was ultimately indicted and impeached in 1988 before he could be recalled. Attempts to reinstate the Holiday via ballot issues lost in 1990. It was ultimately the business community, which went berserk when the National Football League cancelled the planned 1993 Super Bowl, that rallied 61% of the voters to approve the holiday in 1992. Though Arizona then became the first state to officially *pass* the MLK Holiday, the racist image remained.

The horrible plight of Mexican-Americans has been recognized and remembered nationwide due to the notoriety of Cesar Chavez. He was a Yuma farm worker, born in 1927, who led nonviolent farmworker demonstrations, and who formed both the National Farm Workers Association (which later became United Farm Workers).

When I first moved to Phoenix in 1995, things seemed relatively calm compared to the white/Latino conflicts I witnessed in California and New Mexico. But problems escalated during the recession as Sheriff Joe Arpaio appeared often on television, and was lauded as "The Toughest Sheriff in America," when he started raiding businesses and rounding up Latinos. While some of those taken into custody were here illegally, many were not. I will always remember a poor Native American woman being interviewed on television who cried that she had been arrested three times already because the police thought she looked Hispanic.

Things exploded when the Arizona State Legislature, a part-time body, which seldom passed anything of interest, passed State Bill 1070 and it was signed by Governor Jan Brewer in 2010. It was one of the strictest anti-immigration bills in the country. Its restrictions and identification requirements deliberately directed at Mexicans (though people were regularly immigrating, legally and illegally from Canada and other countries) reminded me of the labelling of Jews and homosexuals by the Nazis in WWII.

Arizona became the target of nationwide derision and boycotts, losing $90 million in convention business the first year. International visitors were afraid to come here, and students from other countries were afraid to enroll here. There were demonstrations and marches, money was raised for campaigns to improve Arizona's image, future major sports events were threatened, and business people were apoplexic again.

Ultimately, court decisions derailed most of SB 1070 before it was implemented. Arpaio was voted out of office and convicted of criminal intent for ignoring a Federal judge's order to stop detaining suspected undocumented immigrants, making some Arizonans unhappy. Then he was pardoned by Donald Trump, making more Arizonans unhappy. Trump pushes for the wall; many Arizona officials oppose any more walls. Washington's support of state rights seems arbitrary: good for right-to-life issues, bad for civil rights issues.

As former Arizona director for the BLM, whose land borders the border, I can attest that the wall along the entire border is both impractical and immoral. Wasn't it Republican Ronald Reagan who demanded the Germans "Tear down this wall?" A wall on the Mexican border is no different than the Berlin wall, an artificial separation of families. It is amazing to think that the Great Communicator would not make it through a Republican primary today.

The Capitol Steps are my favorite comedy troupe. I first saw them when a group of Congressional aides started putting on sketches about politics in Washington, DC. in the 1980's. Now, 30+ albums later, these now-professional actors travel around the country and I make it my mission to see them every November at the Scottsdale Center for Performing Arts. One popular skit is "Hotel Arizona," where a Border Patrol agent is hassling a man for his ID. Go see the animated version of it on YouTube https://www.youtube.com/watch?v=4FTLfrzguHk&t=5s to discover the surprise that gets a huge ovation from the Arizona audience when the man says to the agent "I will show you mine if you show me yours."

The Phoenix Indian School was infamous for trying to strip Native Americans of their language and culture since 1892. It was not closed until 1990. There are 21 tribes in Arizona. Though a few tribes (e.g., Navajos, Gila River, Ak-Chin) are prosperous, diabetes and other health issues, alcoholism and accidents have contributed to an average life expectancy for Native Americans in Arizona that is still only 59 years old.

Like burnt toast, all of this history has left a lingering bad odor. It has led many Americans to believe that Arizona is the "whitest state" in America. Businesses, conventions, and general members of the public, especially people of color, have been hesitant to come here. The reality of Phoenix today is…well, it's complicated.

There are the top five myths about Phoenix that impact its image:

1. Arizona is a "White State"

The actual demographics of Phoenix are among the most diverse in the US. While African-Americans remain only around 5%, the overall percentage of ethnic minorities in Phoenix and Tucson is over 50%. The 2017 Phoenix Census figures are 44.4% white, Hispanic 41.8%, Blacks 6.8%, Asian 3.5%, and Native American 2%. Phoenix is already a majority minority city.

2. Arizona is a "Red State"

Though the media always seems to label Arizona a "red state," I have always thought of it as a purple state. The percentage of Republicans is not much greater (about 34%) than Democrats (30%) and barely ahead of Independents, which make up about 34%. During the past 30 years, Arizona has had four Democratic and five Republican governors. Arizona has had numerous women and LBGTQ members in high-level, elected political positions. Bill Clinton carried the state twice. I think Arizonans are more interested in "green" (i.e., money) than red or blue politics.

3. Phoenix is Too Conservative

No, Phoenix is not New York City or San Francisco. But it is no longer thought of as the "Mississippi of the West "(even Mississippi is no longer Mississippi). People are surprised to find out things like Phoenix hosted the first gay chamber in the US. The Greater Phoenix Gay & Lesbian Chamber of Commerce is

over 35 years old and has been the recipient of the National Gay
and Lesbian Chamber of Commerce of the Year Award.

The Phoenix Mayor and Council are bipartisan positions
(though it is usually easy to tell their leanings). For many recent
years, the Black Caucus for the Arizona State Legislature, consisted
of one person—State Senator Leah Landrum, then House
Representative Reginald Bolding. But five others are running
this year. The *Arizona Informant* (the only Black newspaper in
Arizona) held an event to recognize the large number of African-
American candidates running in 2018; over 30 are running for
local, State and Federal seats.

In 2018, Phoenix has scored perfectly on the Human Rights
Campaign's Municipal Equality Index. The City has demonstrated
commitment to enforcing consistent non-discriminatory laws
and practices, offering equal benefits and protections to all as
an employer, and ensuring that all residents are included in City
services and programs.

*4. There are No Minority Businesses or Customers for that
Matter*

When I was trying to create the Greater Phoenix Black
Chamber of Commerce in 1998, the most common question I got
from white people was "What do we need a Black Chamber for?"
Most people could not name one Black-owned business.

In 2012, there were almost 40,000 minority-owned
businesses and over 44,000 women-owned ones. By 2017, there
were 54,000 Hispanic-owned businesses alone. There are over 10
chambers representing and promoting the many ethnic groups
(e.g., Arizona Hispanic Chamber of Commerce, Black Chamber
of Arizona, Asian Corporate & Entrepreneur Leaders, etc.) in

Phoenix. The buying power of minorities is even more impressive; for example, it is over $47 billion today for Hispanics.

5. Reverse Discrimination is the Current Threat

There has been a growing drumbeat, especially since Barack Obama's two-time election, that racial inequality no longer exists. This has led to drives to eliminate scholarships, contracts, training and other methods used to level the playing field for women and minorities.

While some companies have sought to hire more people of color, I never believed there has been any aggressive attempt to share the white-collar pie. Diversity has been promoted primarily in what I refer to as the "cooking and cleaning" sector. Corporations have no problem hiring more people and color for catering or janitorial services, but are not so eager to hire people of color for marketing or accounting or management. Even in the progressive City of Phoenix, while firms are required to submit small business outreach plans and interview diverse business, hiring goals only exist for construction.

On the national level, though women own more than a third of businesses, they were awarded only 5% of the Federal grant money in 2015. Likewise, while the total dollars of Federal grants have been increasing since 2015, the total going to minority owned businesses has not.

In order to practice reverse discrimination, a person or business must have the power to deny employment, contracts or education to those of other races. There just are not enough women and people of color in such positions as CEOs or Board members of Fortune 1000 businesses in Arizona to pose such a threat (or to want to pose a threat) to white males. I think some white males fear people of color will treat them as discriminatorily and badly as they have been treated if they get into power. I have never seen that happen.

There are many talented women and people of color, who are gradually climbing the leadership ladders in Phoenix. They are not bitter; they are not vengeful. I am convinced that they will enhance the future viability of businesses that will be welcoming and successful for residents of all colors, races, national origins, religions, and sexual orientations.

In conclusion, Arizona has had a checkered past. From Japanese internment camps to abuse of Blacks and Hispanics in the fields to segregation, there are many shameful moments and Arizona has shot itself in the foot over and over. While good investigative journalism has helped uncover wrongs, like the VA Hospital crisis, that needed attention, the national media's desire to feed the public's desire for sensationalism and bad news has highlighted Arizona's failures, but not its successes.

Of course, there is still racism in Arizona, like everywhere else. After decades of television advertising, Blacks know more than they need to know about how white people condition their hair, try to remove their wrinkles, tan their skin, plumb their lips, enlarge their breasts and butts, change their eye color with contact lenses, stop their legs from shaking and treat their feet. Meanwhile, as I mentioned earlier, after hundreds of years of supposed co-habitation, white people know…zilch about Black people. There are available sources of information, like Diversityinc.com's "Ask the White Guy" column used to run articles, like "What not to say to an African-American," (e.g. "What did you do to your hair?"). But whites in American have been able to afford not to care.

I still occasionally get followed in high-end stores or am asked for extra identification or am asked if I am in the right line/

seat/place with the other premier, elite or luxury member area. I am sure that some people will pull parts of this book out of context to imply that I am either a reverse racist or an Uncle Tom, a Democrat or a Republican, too aggressive or too submissive, an antagonist or a victim ☺ A friend of mine from England once asked me why Americans always have to categorize people. I was stumped; I did not have an answer. Nothing is black and white. I am all of those and none of them, depending on the day or the hour.

I am saddened to think that, despite a few hopeful moments I have had in my life (e.g., being the first Black valedictorian of PS 45 or one of the two Black women accepted to Cornell University's College of Agriculture of Life Sciences or the first woman field professional hired by BLM or, most recently, the election of the first African-American President), I will not live to see racial or gender equality in the country I love and that my father served a career in the military to protect.

Though currently disappointed, I actually remain optimistic. Yes, after living all over the US, I willingly chose Arizona to be my home for the rest of my life. Weather plays a big factor in why all of us are here. But I also like the potential of Phoenix. As a biologist, I know that hybrids are the most successful plants. The diversity of Phoenix-of its environment, which I worked to preserve, and of its people, whom I work with daily, are very exciting to me. Its future Is as bright as its almost-always blue skies, and I hope you want to be or remain a part of it as much as I do. The rest of this story tells why.

CHAPTER 10
IDOLS AND ICONS

My first week in Phoenix, an official from the City of Scottsdale invited me to an awards luncheon (I was to find out that Phoenicians are very self-congratulatory and have awards events almost weekly). During the event, he nudged me and pointed to the table next to us. "That's Jerry Colangelo," he smiled and whispered. I was soon to find out why he did so with such reverence.

Longtime residents know the legend of how Colangelo arrived in town from Chicago in the 1960's with $76 in his pocket and wound up creating the Phoenix Suns basketball dynasty. You can learn from and about him in his book *How You Play the Game*. He also brought professional baseball to the Valley, mandated players to be involved in the community, was instrumental behind the creation of venues like Chase Field, Comerica Theater, Phoenix Children's Museum, the W Hotel, and renovation of many others. I sincerely believe there would not be a Phoenix, Arizona, today without Jerry Colangelo. His vision, initiative, diligence and compassion are unequaled.

When I next saw him at an event, I went up to reintroduce myself. "I know who you are," he said. As most women, unfortunately, at the time, I was used to being invisible and was shocked that he remembered me. We have had a warm relationship the past 20 years and, though, we would never get a chance to meet for coffee more than once a year, I consider him a mentor and one of the reasons for my success in Arizona.

I was very saddened by the death of the Honorable Senator John McCain in August of this year. I first met him when I was the Deputy Director of BLM in Washington, DC. As a rebel myself, I was quickly drawn to "the Maverick." I was most impressed by his knowledge and appreciation of history, his in-depth study of the issues, and his intellect. During my two terms of service in Washington and many hours of "educating" (in public service, we never "lobby") Congress people, I could tell within the first five minutes whether he/she had any idea or cared what you were talking about. Some were friendly, some were dumb, some were condescending. Senator McCain was always well briefed, respectful, and never let me feel I was beneath him or wasting his time.

Once I got to Arizona, though it was not his top priority (the military and veterans were), McCain had an interest, in public lands. He was supportive of me, the first woman Arizona State Director, and BLM. Together we worked on the legislative language that eventually led to the Arizona Trail being designated as a National Scenic Trail. He defended me when President Clinton and Secretary of the Interior Bruce Babbitt made decisions that the Republicans hated. I defended him when people criticized his temper or coarse sense of humor; after all, that was familiar behavior to a native New Yorker, like myself. Unfortunately, I think Arizona has yet to realize how much funding McCain was responsible for bringing to our state through his support of Luke Air Force Base and development of small and corporate businesses in the State.

I also like and respect his wife, Cindy. She, also, is very intelligent and very committed to doing the right things. One of her main causes was campaigning against sexual exploitation (Sex trafficking is a major problem in Arizona, that is talked about with each major sporting event hosted there, but few are doing anything about). His daughter Meghan is also inspiring. I hope one or both of them pursue political office someday.

I was so proud of how Phoenix handled the memorial arrangements. They were well-organized, dignified and moving. There was even a touch of humor (Frank Sinatra's *My Way* was playing as we exited the church). I was not surprised to later learn that McCain had written all the instructions for the memorial events! You might (or might not by now) be surprised that I, also, have left similar instructions with my will, including that *My Way* be played at my funeral! Sinatra is my all-time favorite performer.

The outpouring of emotion for McCain from throughout Arizona and from all over the country is evidence of the forgiving nature I mentioned earlier. But, in this case, the Senator had more than made up for his transgressions as part of the Keating Five. Sadly, I considered him the last real Republican.

Betsey Bayless' family has been in Arizona for three generations. We were in public service at the same time. Bayless was one of the Fab Five, a group of female politicians who held all the highest offices in the State in the late 1990s. She served as Secretary of State from 1997-2002. Bayless also served on the Maricopa County Board of Supervisors, was CEO of the Maricopa Integrated Health System, and received the Valley Leadership Woman of the Year Award in 2005. I admire Bayless' intelligence, management skills, poise, work ethic and compassion. She also knows how to have fun; we share many interests in common, like baseball, animals and fun photo Christmas cards.

If Martians had landed and looked at an Arizona newsstand (if we still had newsstands), they would think that there are no people of color in the State. If they picked of any of the Phoenix newspaper or magazine collectibles (e.g., 50th Anniversary of…, 30 Years of History…), they might think the only person of color who played any role in the development of Phoenix was basketball star Charles Barkley 30+ years ago. But since its "discovery," people of all races have helped build Phoenix and Arizona. So, I want to pay tribute to some of them.

Historically, I do not think the Buffalo Soldiers have gotten their due. Blacks played a major role in the West, both as soldiers and cowboys, that was totally neglected by Hollywood and television. Henry Flipper, the first African-American graduate of the U.S. Military Academy, actually served at Ft Huachuca in southern Arizona. While with BLM, I got to help preserve buildings and artifacts re: the 9th and 10th US Calvary in Arizona and New Mexico. My interest dates back to my childhood (my father had been a *real* Black cowboy as a young man; he grew up on a ranch in Texas). I was thrilled to meet Danny Glover during the making of the 1997 Buffalo Soldiers movie, which was filmed on BLM public lands near Benson.

I encourage you to do your own research to better understand how Phoenix and Arizona developed and who helped make it happen. You are not likely to learn much in traditional history books. But examples of where you can go include *The First 100 Years: A History of Blacks in Arizona* by Richard E Harris or *Race Work: The Rise of Civil Rights in the Urban West* by Dr Matthew Whitaker, CEO of Diamond Strategies, who is a noted historian in Phoenix.

As the first Black member of the Arizona State Legislature, Cloves Campbell Sr helped pass legislation mandating that required Arizona textbooks include the accomplishments of people of color. He died in 2004. I hope the legacy of him and his family are documented in future texts. Among his many lasting influences, was *The Arizona Informant*, the only statewide newspaper documenting activities in the Black community, which continues to be published by his grandson Cloves Campbell III.

Dr. Morrison Warren became the first Black Phoenix City Councilman in 1966. I have had the honor of knowing Calvin Goode, who served as the second and only African-American Phoenix Councilman for 22 years and 11 terms (1972-1994). Today, at 91, he amazingly continues to be an advocate for jobs and job training, education, youth programs, women- and minority-owned businesses, LBGTQ rights, the Carver School Museum, and other issues he championed while on the Council.

Congressman Ed Pastor, like Senator McCain, was responsible for campaigning for a lot of resources to Arizona. We probably would not have the light rail or road systems we have without him. This Arizona native was the first Latino to serve Arizona in Congress; he served in the House of Representatives from 1991-2015. He had previously served on the Maricopa Board of Supervisors. Pastor was a fervent supporter of progressive issues (e.g., pro-choice, anti-war, gun control, wildlife protection, civil rights, etc.) that were not always popular in Arizona. But he was always popular, easily winning re-elections. I liked his honesty and passion for protecting underserved populations. He is still an active alumnus with his alma mater—ASU. His daughter, Laura, currently serves on the Phoenix City Council.

Ronnie Lopez is a consultant, who is also a native of Arizona. He and I both worked for Secretary of Interior Bruce Babbitt during the Clinton Administration. He had served Babbitt previously as Chief of Staff and worked with him when Babbitt ran for President. Lopez is a lifelong advocate of human rights; he worked for the Arizona Civil Rights Commission, served as a Justice of the Peace, and was President/Chief Executive Officer of Chicanos Por La Causa. I admire all he has done for the community, by not only helping many politicians, but by serving on innumerable boards and commissions. I also was friends with his son Paul, who we tragically lost this year, and with whom I worked on some consulting projects.

I know it might look like I only network with politicians. That is not the case. But I do associate with and admire great leaders. We need to identify, recognize and support more leaders, who are both experts in their fields, dedicated to helping people in the community, and have the ability to impact the lives of millions.

I also want to let all entrepreneurs know that there are many wonderful leaders in Phoenix, who are not as famous, who do not get the recognition that they deserve, but who have acted as and can be excellent mentors and role models of how to be an effective businessperson. It is sad that many do not know about the diverse talent right here in the Valley.

Some people include **Harry Garewal**, who served as a successful CEO of the Hispanic Chamber of Commerce for six years and is known nationwide for his advocacy work with education and Hispanic-American issues; **Vada Manager**, who is a brilliant international business consultant and previous executive with Nike; **Kim Covington**—who was a television broadcaster for many years before becoming an executive with the Arizona Community Foundation; **Hassan Abdul-Kareem**-one of the first Black executives on Wall Street, now is CEO of Brotha Love Productions-a music management company—and a professional sports photographer; **Lynn Austin**—a previous executive with Harley Davidson and Ford, who is now a professor, author and public speaker, helping people overcome personal hardships; **Dr. George Brooks Jr,** who is a speaker, writer, environmentalist and President/CEO of NxT Horizon, an Ag Tech (Agriculture Technology) consulting firm focusing on sustainable solutions; **Diana Gregory**, a former executive with Budweiser, who established Gregory's Fresh Market, a wonderful non-profit that promotes healthy eating among seniors; **Benito Almanza**, who went from a childhood of working in the fields with his migrant family to becoming the Arizona President of Bank of America; **Abraham James**, one of the fewer than 10 Black architects in Arizona, who has successfully run the monthly Greater Green Gables Neighborhood meetings in Phoenix for years; **Deb Morgaina**, now retired, who built and ran Balanced Business Consulting, helping innumerable corporations and small businesses in Phoenix get organized for 25 years; and **Jean Fairfax,** the lifelong educator who passed away at 98 years of age, and, with her sister Betty, became legendary for philanthropy which provided scholarships and supported civil rights in Phoenix.

Since I have over 1000 people on Facebook and over 4000 on LinkedIn, there are many more people I could (and probably should) mention. But I just wanted to demonstrate a sample of the breadth and depth of the idols and icons we have here in Phoenix, who have not only created and succeeded at their own businesses, but have dedicated themselves to helping other businesses, non-profits, and the community. If you are already here or moving to Phoenix, you are or will be in good company.

These are two long-time Arizonans—Jerry Colangelo and Senator John McCain—

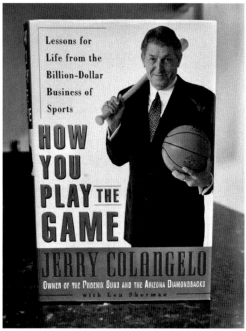

who served as mentors and role models for me and innumerable others in Phoenix. It is hard to imagine what Phoenix would have been today without their vision, commitment, and leadership.

I could fill an encyclopedia (if we still had encyclopedias) with the many wonderful men and women that have, not just made Phoenix their home, but have helped create a beautiful city that respects people of every race, color, religion, sexual orientation, national origin and age for future generations. Here are just some of the many ones I have had the blessing to know and, hopefully, you get to meet.

CHAPTER 11
RISING FROM THE ASHES

"In Greek mythology (https://en.wikipedia.org/wiki/Greek_mythology), a phoenix is a long-lived bird (https://en.wikipedia.org/wiki/Bird) that cyclically regenerates or is otherwise born again. Associated with the Sun, a phoenix obtains new life by arising from the ashes (https://en.wikipedia.org/wiki/Ash) of its predecessor. According to some sources, the phoenix dies in a show of flames and combustion, although there are other sources that claim that the legendary bird dies and simply decomposes before being born again." Van der Broek, R (1972), The Myth of the Phoenix, Seeger, I trans, EJ Brill

I guess in the case of the Phoenix in Arizona, the bird totally decomposed. At the height (or depth) of the recession (2007-2012), deserted strip malls, empty store fronts, abandoned housing and office tower developments littered the Phoenix landscape. Phoenix crashed the hardest and recovered the most slowly in the country. But, like the bird after which it is named, Phoenix has been reborn and risen from the ashes.

According to the Census Bureau, in 2017, Phoenix was the second fastest-growing large US city in 2017, just behind San Antonio. Most people in other parts of the US are surprised when I tell them Phoenix is now the 5th largest city in the nation and is supposed to rise to #4 by 2020. Warm weather, no natural disasters, low taxes and reasonable cost of living are magnets for those from Detroit, Los Angeles, Chicago, Seattle, and Canada. There are many other reasons for people from anywhere to move families and/or businesses here to become a part of the expected 6.3 million population in the Phoenix Metropolitan Area by 2030.

What I like most about Phoenix is its options!

As I already mentioned, you can live close to downtown or on the edge of a desert preserve. With the prevalence of coop working spaces and online virtual offices, you do not have to venture far from your bedroom to go to work. There are new housing and apartments at all price levels.

Phoenix now appeals to all ages. Historically, Phoenix was a place for people to come to heal or retire. With state-of-the-art medical facilities like the Mayo Clinic, Barrow's Neurological Center and Phoenix Children's Hospital, it is still a preferred medical location for patients from all over the world. Huge retirement communities, like Sun City and Sun City West, continue to cater to senior citizens.

But demographics have changed dramatically overall for our area. For example, Mesa used to be a small quiet place, originally was inhabited by the Hohokam natives thousands of years ago, that was primarily for senior citizens, heavily Mormon. It is now, at over 400,000 people, one of the most densely populated areas in the State with over 47% Hispanic, Black and other races, almost 60% under 44, and only 13% over the age of 65. VisitMesa's social media campaigns heavily target young people to new bars, restaurants, wineries and entertainment venues.

The plethora of leisure opportunities is one of the reasons I picked Arizona as my last stop. If you are a couch potato, you can lay in your hammock in the backyard all year. But if you are active, there is a wide range of options.

Then-Secretary of Interior Bruce Babbitt said he was glad to see me transfer to his home state because I was good at handling transitions and the four of the five C's (cotton, cattle, citrus, copper), that had supported its economy, were disappearing. With climate still an asset, he thought I could help Arizona make the transition to new priorities, like recreation.

When I arrived in Arizona, one of the first things I did was co-found the Arizona Tourism Alliance to help bring all sectors of the tourism industry (hotels, rental cars, restaurants, etc.) together to stop competing and start working together to promote the State.

During Babbitt's tenure in Washington, we were able to designate four National Monuments, the Arizona National Scenic Trail, and many special areas, while still enhancing facilities for off-highway vehicle users, mountain bikers, hunters, RVers, and other users of public lands. Outdoor activities range from boating (yes, there are some spectacular lakes throughout Arizona) to skiing (e.g., Snowball) in the north and bird watching (e.g., Sierra Vista) in the south.

If the only image one had of Phoenix is what he/she saw on television or in the movies, "culture" would not probably come to mind. But, especially since the recovery, it is easy to go to a play, concert, ballet, symphony, stand-up comedy, or opera every week. The venues in Phoenix are all refurbished or new. Prices are much more reasonable that LA, Vegas or New York. The performers are talented and enthusiastic.

Regarding educational options, Phoenix is bi-polar with a poor primary school system and outstanding secondary school one. K-12 education remains a problem, an inexcusable one. It is the Achilles heel of the State. Arizona always seems to be in competition for last place in the US. I think in the old days, education was not a priority because Phoenix was a retirement community; there were no kids to worry about. Then, I think Phoenix was overwhelmed when building schools and hiring teachers could not keep pace with the number of families suddenly moving here before the recession.

Now, that fund are scarce, I am afraid, education is not the priority it should be because the public school system is filled with mainly Hispanic- and African-American children. Until enough people vote enough people into office, who care, the only option for some families is to seek out private schools or public schools in the several excellent school districts in Phoenix.

In sharp contrast, Phoenix has a unique and excellent college-level school system. Michael Crow arrived from Columbia University in 2002 and shocked Arizonans by boldly telling them that Arizona State University (ASU) was a third-tier university, but that he could change that. Dr. Crow has delivered. ASU has been voted the Most Innovative University for several years in a row. Because Arizona only has three state universities and there is an unusual and historic lack of other private colleges, ASU has swelled to over 80,000 students and is one of the largest public universities in the country.

ASU has excellent and unique schools (e.g., the WP Carey School of Business, the Walter Cronkite School of Communication and the College of Public Service & Community Solutions, which was just renamed after Michael and Cindy Watts who donated $30 million). It also has outstanding new facilities, including the Sandra Day O'Connor College of Law and the remodeled Sun Devil Stadium.

In addition to improvements in the programs, research and venues, and growth in the student body, Crow has ensured that the student body, of what he refers to as the New American University model, is a diverse one in every way—ethnicity, geographically, economically, gender, sexual orientation, and talent.

Soon after I moved to Phoenix, Grand Canyon was a little Baptist-affiliated university, ensconced in scandal and on the verge of bankruptcy. Today it is a non-profit, multi-faith university with over 19,000 students. Over $1 billion has been spent in the last ten years to invest in new dorms, a state-of-the-art STEM center, more faculty, a fabulous stadium and arena and more. GCU has also made it a priority to interact with people in the surrounding West Phoenix community.

Again, outstanding leadership from people like Brian Mueller, the hyper-energetic change agent and President since 2009, who electrifies every room he walks into; long-time administrator Faith Weese, the Chief University Relations Officer, who has been nurturing interactions with the community for over 30 years, and the newer Dan Marjele, a hometown sports hero, who is ushering the Lopes basketball team to new heights of performance and attendance. Oh, yeah, Jerry Colangelo is the muse behind the Colangelo College of Business at GCU, too.

One way that Phoenix stands out from many other cities is the abundance of professional sports. Phoenix has them all: MLB's Arizona Diamondbacks, WNBA's Phoenix Mercury and NBA's Phoenix Suns (thanks, originally, to Jerry Colangelo), NFL's Arizona Cardinals, arena football's Arizona Rattlers, and NHL's Arizona Coyotes. One can go to see a professional sport in a nice inside stadium any time of year. As importantly to local businesses, as a result of its nice weather and newer facilities, the Phoenix Metropolitan area is often chosen to host the major sports events (e.g., the State Farm Stadium has had two Super Bowl's and annually hosts the Fiesta Bowl). These games contribute hundreds of thousands of dollars to the economy when they arrive.

In addition to these sports, Arizona has become a mecca for baseball's spring training teams. New stadiums, no rain delays and proximity to hotels and restaurants has drawn teams to our Cactus League from Florida's Grapefruit League. Many tourists come and stay the whole month of March to see their favorite teams from Kansas City, Milwaukee, Chicago, etc. Even the DBacks moved their spring training from Tucson to Salt River Fields in Scottsdale.

There are still some challenges facing the sports industry in Arizona. Being relatively new, Phoenix teams do not have the historical (and sometimes fanatical) fan base of other teams. Though it is getting better, many of the fans in the stands are still those rooting for the teams from the places they used to live. Also, locals tend to turn out only when teams are doing well and, unfortunately, that is not too common. The Mercury and Rattlers have been good, and the Cardinals went to the Super Bowl in 2009, but the 2001 Arizona Diamondbacks are the only one of the major four sports to win a national championship. There is still some uncertainty about the future of the Coyotes who are on a year-to-year lease in the Gila River Arena in Glendale, Arizona, and both the Suns and DBacks are murmuring about needing new stadiums.

Not to be forgotten is America's top spectator sport—NASCAR. The 51-year-old Phoenix International Raceway (PIR) just finished a $178 million renovation and renaming (it is now ISM Raceway due to the naming rights purchased by the tech company ISM Connect). Again, Phoenix is unique in that it hosts two NASCAR weekends a year, one of which is the Monster Energy NASCAR cup semi-final race. As a journalist, event planner and youth sports advocate, I worked with former PIR CEO Bryan

Sperber to document the physical and social evolution of the track since his arrival in 2002. The track has consistently brought in $400 million annually to the local economy, as 6000 RVs filled its lots and fans filled Phoenix hotels twice a year. With enhanced facilities, new CEO Julie Giese, and now as host of the final race of the NASCAR Chase, no telling how much ISM Raceway can contribute to the future Arizona economy..

As a native New Yorker, I can admit that we New Yorkers love to complain. As Phoenix' cultural offerings have improved (the Phoenix Zoo, Desert Botanical Gardens, Phoenix Art Museum, Heard Museum, Arizona Science Center, MIM and other attractions have enhanced their venues and programs), the complaints have died down the past 10 years …except for one issue. If you put two New Yorkers together in Phoenix, within the first five minutes, the conversation turns to good food or how you can't find any here. But even that is starting to change.

CHAPTER 12
HOPE FOR FOODIES

Many US cities are famous for a certain cuisine or dish:

◊   Dallas & Kansas City for BBQ

◊   New Orleans for beignets

◊   Portland for Dungeness crabs

◊   Baltimore for blue crabs

◊   The old Las Vegas for shrimp cocktails

◊   Santa Fe for Mexican food

◊   San Francisco for chocolates

◊   Milwaukee for cheese

◊   Honolulu for mahi mahi

◊   New York City for Jewish delis

◊   Austin for TexMex

Phoenix is famous for…nothing really. I have always been puzzled why Phoenix does not have some specialty, e.g., at least Mexican food in a state, where over a third of the population is Hispanic. If you get any two New Yorkers together in Phoenix, within five minutes they are talking about where they can find decent lasagna.

Phoenix has had some excellent luxury restaurants in the past (e.g., Michael's). It has some historic steakhouses, like Durant's and the Stockyards, that are fun. I have a few favorites—Jade Palace for Chinese food (the owners cook it NY style and 80% of their customers are from NYC) or Tomás for Italian food, and NYPD Pizza is as close as I have come to the real thing. But I have hesitated to mention my favorite restaurants in the past, as it seemed like a curse as they began to close up. Even famous, successful chains, e.g., McCormick's & Schmick's and Kincaid's, packed up and left town.

There are many theories about why Phoenix had "failed at food" and restaurants were not frequented, including its residents' casualness, the low Arizona wages for both customers and servers, the recession, few famous chefs living here, lack of diversity (Washington DC's proliferation of embassies helps inspire all types of international cuisines), and the traditional excuse for everything that is wrong with Phoenix: "it's too hot to go out." High-end restaurants became sites for only special occasions, and restaurants cannot survive on people coming once a year.

The place that was the most depressing representation of our lack of identity was Sky Harbor International Airport. In Boston's Logan International Airport, you could enjoy a great bowl of New England clam chowder. Not that you had time while you were running through the terminals, but if you did, your choices in Phoenix, were chain-store pre-made pizza or nuked burgers at inflated prices.

Good food is important for entrepreneurs in several ways. Since the disappearance of meals on planes, it is helpful to be able to grab a good to-go meal in the airport on your way to your conference or when you arrive back from home from a conference, too tired to think about cooking dinner, before you get your Uber.

For over 15 years, in my consulting business, I have recruited small businesses and helped them compete for food and retail concessions at Sky Harbor. During the most recent reconstruction of the terminals at the airport, Phoenix has made a special effort to encourage local, unique restaurants to apply. As a result, though there is still no general theme, there are now Phoenix favorites, like LoLo's Chicken & Waffles, available which travelers will probably not experience in other airports.

Well-fed employees are happy employees. It helps recruitment, retention and morale to have decent places for employees to have a decent meal within a short time frame at lunchtime. That has not always been possible in the past in Phoenix. Either there were no nearby restaurants, or the only options were clusters of high-calorie, poor-quality fast food.

Phoenix's recovery has led to a literal explosion of restaurants in all areas of the city. Younger people, people arriving from cities with good restaurant cultures, and more ethnicities bringing their habits and cultures with them, are seeking new, innovative, healthier places to eat.

There are now complexes of good restaurants near employment centers in Scottsdale Quarter, Mill Avenue in Tempe, Kierland in North Phoenix, downtown Glendale, and Gilbert Restaurant Row. During the past couple of years, in a 7th

Street Central Phoenix corridor bordered by Bethany Home and Missouri Ave, old buildings have been remodeled into a slew of new restaurants that have attracted the top developers, like Fox, and celebrity chefs. It is impossible to count all the new quick service spots in downtown Phoenix, which have opened to serve thousands of hungry and health-conscious college students. VisitMesa and Experience Scottsdale have developed entire marketing campaigns and maps to promote their foodie and wine tours.

Another need of entrepreneurs are places to take clients and have business meetings. It used to be very difficult to find a full-service restaurant where you could hear your guest above loud music or boisterous diners. Biltmore Fashion Park, which continues to evolve, has hot dogs and tacos, but you can also schedule a sure-to-please lunch in upscale settings at Seasons 52 or The Capital Grille. A tried-and-true, but seemingly unknown gem to newcomers, is the old Compass Restaurant in the downtown Hyatt. Your guests will be impressed by the beautiful night-time views of the city as tower with your dining table rotates. But you can also entertain your clients at one of the newer upscale restaurants, like the classy Blue Hound Kitchen and Cocktails, in CityScape.

Yes, our Southwest rival Las Vegas transformed itself from cheap shrimp cocktails and steak & egg breakfasts into a fine-dining haven years ago. But Phoenix, though it does not have a city forte like cheesesteak subs of its own, is on its way to becoming a huge and exciting potpourri of modern and unique restaurants.

CHAPTER 13
THE RUSH HOUR

Two issues that might affect your choice of site for growing your business (and may have irrationally affected mine) are weather and traffic. I have already discussed weather…in its extremes. I had been traumatized by parents having to battle blizzards to come rescue me from schools as a child to having to wait for neighbors to dig you out of your house half buried by snow. So, living in Phoenix, the thought of never having to scrape another car windshield or wait for the car to warm up or shovel the car out after the snow plow comes down the street is sweet. Another relief is traffic or lack thereof.

Most major cities have a central core where commercial, political and societal leaders congregate and from which they run the empire. Such was the case of the two cities where I have spent half of my life: Washington, DC and New York City.

Washington, DC, of course, is not just the heartbeat of a city, but the Capitol of the country. Spectacularly huge historic buildings and monuments house about a million workers during the week. People can walk a few blocks in any direction, get a bus or subway, and reach any place they need to go in the 60 square miles of the District. I loved living within walking distance of Metrorail trains, which arrived every six minutes, or a twenty-minute drive through beautiful Rock Creek park to work on C Street. But many people commuted as long as two hours each way via bumper-to-bumper traffic or commuter railroads from surrounding states to work in DC.

Throughout history, the entire borough of Manhattan has been considered the "downtown" of New York City. One of the thrills in life is to fly into LaGuardia Airport on a clear day and gasp at the site of over a hundred buildings over 500 feet tall seeming to rise from the water surrounding this tiny 22 square foot island. While there are people, who commute by car from New Jersey and the other neighboring boroughs and states, I grew up, as most people there did, believing that owning a car was not just impractical; it was idiotic.

Gas stations are scarce, insurance and parking rates, are outrageous (in 2017, the NYC Parking Authority reported that the average monthly cost of parking in the city was over $400!), and there are ridiculous rules (e.g., alternate side-of-the-street parking regulations require some people to move their cars every day).

The rush hours in both cities run from around 5:30 AM to 10 AM. Therefore, throughout my career, though I love cars, I hate driving and have always lived near work (the twenty-minute commute by car in DC was probably the farthest).

When I moved to Phoenix in 1995, it was a small city (about a million residents) that acted like a small town. I used to joke that if you have the Mayor's home phone number, you live in a small town. The metropolitan areas has since grown to over four million and is the fifth largest city in the US. But there are several things that make it very unique and a wonderful place to work and run a business.

Not many major corporations have headquarters in the Phoenix Metropolitan area. The few (e.g., utility companies like

APS and SRP or tech companies like Motorola or Intel) that do struggle to support the charities and cultural amenities, like the Symphony and Ballet that city residents expect. Phoenix is also the largest city geographically in the US (over 500 square miles!). But there is no concentrated area of corporate or government complexes attracting hundreds of thousands of workers.

I joke with people that I am a "B-51," that is I lived in Phoenix before State Route 51. Until the late 1990's, there were only two highways (I-10 and I-17) along the south and west edges of town. Left turn signals were very rare. Even when the 51 (1/2 mile from my house) opened, it only went from downtown to Shea Blvd., and most of the senior citizens would not get on it.

It is hard to believe that, in twenty years, an incredible, and sometimes confusing, web of highways (State Routes 101, 202, 303, etc.) have sent Phoenix sprawling in all directions. One thing that I have not seen elsewhere Is that Arizona will not just close some lanes on these major highways, but close all of them, from time to time for repairs. So, you need to pay close attention to construction notices.

But those of us who have lived in NYC or LA or DC laugh when people in Phoenix complain about the traffic. Rush hour in Phoenix is an hour, about 5 to 6 PM, versus the four-hour rush hours in some other cities.

Also, unlike most big cities, you still have the option of living close in or farther out, with easy access to a major highway or easy ways to avoid them, to commute or not to commute. One of the best assets about Phoenix is its air access. Both American Airlines and Southwest Airlines have major hubs at Sky Harbor International Airport, which is only 15 minutes from downtown Phoenix. Compare that to the journey one must make from Denver to Denver International Airport.

In 1996, when I decided to move the Arizona State Office of the Bureau of Land Management and its two hundred employees four miles to a newly remodeled building on Central Avenue in downtown Phoenix, I almost had a mutiny. Some people, who grew up in Phoenix had not ever been downtown, and those residents who had visited downtown did not want to go back. Not having been downtown previously I have no idea what it was like, but it must have been pretty scary. But it had started to be cleaned up by the time I arrived in Phoenix and, once we got into the attractive new space with nearby restaurants and conveniences, employees were pleasantly surprised and content.

Today, "Downtown Phoenix," as it is referred to after many aborted attempts (e.g., Copper Square) to label it, is the area between 7th Street and 7th Avenue, from McDowell Road on the north to Buckeye Road on the south. Phoenix is now bustling with new bars, restaurants, condos and offices. The city streets are clean, parking is plentiful and relatively inexpensive (for the moment), and the rush hour is an hour (5-6 PM)!

Phoenix is an exciting and welcoming place for small businesses. While working from home is booming (visualize running your company from your laptop as you sit by your pool in January), there are also many new, convenient and inexpensive coop spaces throughout the Valley. You can rent a room for one day or every day during the month with access to WiFi, conference rooms and kitchens for lunchmaking.

Still not having a central area of high-rises for big corporations, Phoenix has made other interesting accommodations. The City of Phoenix, Arizona State University (ASU) and the University of Arizona (UofA) colluded (in the good sense of the word!) to create a campus in the downtown area. In 2006, ASU's College of Public Programs moved from Tempe, Arizona, to the area. Since that time, other colleges (like ASU's Sandra Day O'Connor Law School and the UofA College of Medicine) have taken over vacant buildings and constructed new ones, relocating programs and their students there.

Most cities use the philosophy of "if we build it (e.g., new stadium), they will come." In Phoenix, the opposite approach has worked. Phoenix placed tens of thousands of students downtown and the businesses (restaurants, entertainment, a grocery store, apartments, and other servicing companies) followed!

Another way Phoenix has adapted to a large surface area is to replicate services all over the Valley. The metropolitan area is a conglomeration of cities in Maricopa and Pinal counties. The best-known cities are Phoenix, Scottsdale, Glendale, Chandler, Mesa, and Tempe. But the post-recession booming populations of Gilbert, Peoria, Surprise and Goodyear have broadened the favorable areas for new businesses.

The City of Phoenix, itself, is a collection of 15 "villages," geographically and politically. Many newcomers do not even realize that they are in one of the following villages:

◊   Ahwatukee Foothills

◊   Alhambra

◊   Camelback East

◊   Central City

◊   Deer Valley

◊   Desert View

◊   Encanto

◊   Estrella

◊   Laveen

◊   Maryvale

◊   North Gateway

◊   North Mountain

◊   Paradise Valley

◊   Rio Vista, and

◊   South Mountain

Confusing? Yes! On one hand, this means there are a lot of different mayors, councils, planning committees, permitting procedures, budget schedules and other challenges of which corporations and small businesses need to be aware. You need to do a lot of research before you decide where to locate your business to determine what set of taxes, regulations, target employees and audiences, accessible suppliers, and other factors are most beneficial to your particular goods or services.

On the other hand, this means that you do not necessarily need to travel far to go to work, shop or get services. Shopping, restaurant, business and entertainment centers are duplicated throughout the metropolitan area. The good news is that there is a plethora of wonderful locations and opportunities available to all types of businesses, large and small.

https://www.azcentral.com/story/news/local/ phoenix/2017/06/11/phoenix-nation-5th-largest-but-real-city/369917001/

EPILOGUE

IT TAKES A VILLAGE TO KILL A ROOF RAT, BUT WHY WE LIVE HERE

One might think you could just set a mouse trap and be done with it. Actually, I needed an army of supporters to deal with the roof rat. The survival tip I have for entrepreneurs that encounter this epidemic is that It takes a village to kill a roof rat.

One might think you could just set a mouse trap and be done with it. Actually, I needed an army of supporters to deal with the roof rat.

"That's why the dishwasher is not working," the repairman said, stating the new obvious. He had to completely replace the under-counter dishwasher, whose plastic housing was chewed through in several places. But that may have saved my house burning down, as that model was later recalled for starting fires.

The next day, I had to hire an animal control specialist, since there is usually more than one roof rat. He set some traps under the dishwasher and in the cabinet, in case roof rat #1 returned to the scene of the crime, and, eventually screened off the chimney and every possible orifice to the house.

My ideal neighbor—Gary Young—had to help me dispose of roof rat #1, when we heard the loud snap of the trap (yes, he did return) later that day.

The manager at the local hardware store had to give me advice on the best poison to place in the backyard to quickly kill the roof rats, without upsetting the delicate balance of my backyard, which included a variety of birds and my cairn terrier.

Speaking of my Cairn, I had to consult my dog handler to see why my show dog terrier, a breed bred to kill rats, had, instead fled in terror from the kitchen the night before the repairman arrived. "If he had seen the rat, he probably would have killed it," he explained. "But all he saw was a shaking dishwasher monster." I guess that made sense. That *would* be scary to anyone.

Scarier is the expense of removing the rats. The roof rat epidemic hit Ahwatukee, a suburban area of Phoenix, first, but has now spread to other areas. Roof rats frequent areas with trees of their favorite food—citrus fruit. When relocating to Phoenix, inquire about the issue in your new neighborhood. If you are already here, attack the problem early before you need to start replacing appliances.

The poison, traps and screening certainly helped. But what I think ultimately eliminated the rats was something very simple, very natural: cats. A couple of feral cats came into the neighborhood. One piece of advice that I often give entrepreneurs and the one that I will end on is not even original. It is an old adage: "KISS: Keep it Simple, Stupid."

The answer to a problem is often very obvious, right under our noses. Just like in baseball, sometimes we let the analytics get in the way of common sense. If the pitcher is doing well, let him keep pitching, no matter how many pitches he has made so far, and analytics guy is telling you no one should make more than 100 pitches.

Cats kill rats. They love to kill rats. Invite them in to kill rats. Cities throughout the US are purposely releasing spayed feral cats in infested areas. I know environmentalists complain about the ecological balance, how cats also kill birds, blah, blah, blah. But most of these people probably have not encountered roof rats. Maybe I just had quicker, smarter birds in my backyard then. But my collection of doves, pigeons, grackles and hummingbirds were not impacted by the cats.

There was one tabby Gary and I really liked. He was very friendly and efficient. I gave him a lot of credit for resolving my problem and was very sad when he eventually got killed by a car (disadvantage of having a *feral* cat).

Phoenix is a great place for entrepreneurs because things here are simple. The sun comes up almost every single day. So, in the winter, there is no need to remember to buy a new snow shovel, stock salt or decide whether or not to try to get to work or figure out your Plan B method of getting there if you do decide to go. No umbrellas, warming up the car, no shoveling the driveway. Scratch "weather" off your list of things to worry about.

Your commute to work in Phoenix can be as simple or as complicated as you want it to be.

The suggested solutions for avoiding or mitigating burrs and other annoyances I described are simple…compared to evacuating from or rebuilding after tornados or hurricanes.

The scoundrels you might encounter here are amateurs compared to the Madoff copycats on Wall Street or the Weinstein clones in LA.

You can do a lot better than survive in Phoenix; any entrepreneur with a decent education and a little ambition, who values diversity and common sense, and who does not mind that A + B may not =C here, can thrive in Phoenix. When I was a teenager, there was a famous Alka-Seltzer (if anyone remembers what that it was) commercial with the punchline "Try it, you'll like it." I recommend you try Phoenix, you'll *love* it.

I included this old, faded photo to honor my family. It was one of the last of the whole family together in the 1970's. Both my parents were only children, they only had two children, and I came along very late (and probably, surprisingly!) and have no children. So you can see it has always been a very small group. My parents Glenarva and Dorothy Meridith and older sister Rosa Scott are gone now. My niece Robin lives in Chicago and my nephew Raymond Scott Jr. and his family are in Dallas. I am blessed and proud to say that my family was my foundation, why I am what I am today. My last piece of advice to entrepreneurs is, even if your life was not as lucky as mine, remember where you came from, and how you can either use those lessons—good or bad—to overcome the roof rats of life on your way to success.

APPENDIX
WHERE DID YOU HEAR THAT
(REFERENCES)

In the past, whenever I was asked what I wanted to achieve as a writer, I had two objectives. My first goal was to have someone *say*, after reading any of my now over 1000 articles or 10 years of blogs "I didn't know that!" I will have hit a home run (yes, I know, I use to many sports analogies) if someone *thinks* "I want to learn more about that."

When I first started writing this book, I regressed into my professional biologist mindset and began writing footnotes. Then I realized that most people do not know what a footnote is anymore, much less care about reading one. So many get their news anymore from Trump's 400-pound guy in the basement. But I hope, after you have read this book, you are curious and want to check out some of these publications, articles and videos (and many more on your own) to find out more about some of these serious (and some not so serious) issues. *No* news is objective anymore. Keep searching for the truth!

Publications (The news that's still fit to read!)

Most newspapers now seem to just download articles from UP or

AP. These are nationwide publications will get *me* to say "I didn't know that!"

NY Times https://www.nytimes.com
Washington Post https://www.washingtonpost.com
Diversityinc.com https://www.diversityinc.com

Arizona Natural & Unnatural Disasters

Learn More about Burr Medic and Its Control
https://www.gardeningknowhow.com/plant-problems/weeds/
burr-medic-weed.htm

This is why dust storms are called 'haboobs' in Arizona
https://www.azcentral.com/story/news/local/arizona-
weather/2018/07/10/haboob-definition-meaning-name-dust-
storm-wind-monsoon/770406002/

Arizona political scandals back in focus with investigations by Dan
Nowicki- May. 19, 2012 The Republic | azcentral.com
http://archive.azcentral.com/arizonarepublic/news/
articles/20120519arizona-political-scandals.html

Trump in Arizona

Trump International Hotel & Residence
https://en.wikipedia.org/wiki/Trump_International_Hotel_%26_
Residence

City Panel Rejects Height on Trump Hotel
https://www.bizjournals.com/phoenix/stories/2005/02/28/
daily57.html

<u>Diversity in Arizona</u>

A look at black history and segregation in Phoenix by Brandon Lee
https://www.msn.com/en-us/sports/nba/dallas-mavericks-at-phoenix-suns/game-center/sp-id-30401000002074665??ocid=ocid=INSSPBD10

Race Work: The Rise of Civil Rights in the Urban West (Race and Ethnicity in the American West) by Matthew C. Whitaker (https://www.amazon.com/Matthew-C.-Whitaker/e/B001JRUW7E/ref=sr_ntt_srch_lnk_1?qid=1539871043&sr=8-1)
https://www.amazon.com/Race-Work-Rights-Ethnicity-American-ebook/dp/B003PDOMLW/ref=sr_1_1?ie=UTF8&qid=1539871043&sr=8-1&keywords=matthew+whitaker+Phoenix

Capitol Steps Immigration Song-Arizona Hotel
YouTube
https://www.youtube.com/watch?v=4FTLfrzguHk&t=6s

Minorities Now in the Majority in Phoenix and Tucson
https://tucson.com/news/minorities-now-in-the-majority-in-phoenix-and-tucson/article_801a07f0-a45b-5d22-8158-62a47c0105dc.html

Projection of Total Black Buying Power by State (Date from the Selig Center's study, Multicultural Economy, 2004, Table 5, p. 20)
http://blackwallstreet.org/news.coverage.articles.reports/8800000000008885.html

Hispanic Buying Power in Arizona Will Surpass 57 billion by 2022
https://azbigmedia.com/hispanic-buying-power-in-arizona-will-surpass-57-billion-by-2022/

Women- and minority-owned businesses receive only a small fraction of federal contracts
By Megan Janetsky April 13, 2018
https://www.opensecrets.org/news/2018/04/women-owned-biz-receive-fraction-of-fed-contracts/

Arizona Informant http://azinformant.com
Phxsoul.com https://www.phxsoul.com

Arizona Recession and Recovery

Economy of Phoenix
https://en.wikipedia.org/wiki/Economy_of_Phoenix

The Top 5 Reasons Why S.B. 1070—and Laws Like It—Cause Economic Harm
https://www.americanprogress.org/issues/immigration/news/2012/06/25/11677/the-top-5-reasons-why-s-b-1070-and-laws-like-it-cause-economic-harm/

Arizona's once-feared immigration law, SB 1070, loses most of its power in settlement
http://www.latimes.com/nation/la-na-arizona-law-20160915-snap-story.html

At last, Arizona recovers from Great Recession
https://www.bizjournals.com/phoenix/stories/2005/02/28/daily57.html

Phoenix, Buckeye among fastest-growing U.S. cities in 2017 by Dani Coble, Cronkite News. May 30, 2018 https://www.azcentral.com/story/news/local/southwest-valley/2018/05/30/phoenix-buckeye-among-fastest-growing-cities-nationwide/656562002/

ABOUT THE AUTHOR...

DENISE P. MERIDITH

Denise P. Meridith is currently the CEO/President of Denise Meridith Consultants Inc. (DMCI), a community and public relations firm. This New York native served 29 years in the Federal government. After being the first professional woman hired by the Bureau of Land Management (BLM), she had many management positions in six states, and became the first woman BLM Deputy Director in Washington, DC in 1992. She retired early from BLM after serving seven years as the Arizona State Director, where she managed 14 million acres of public lands, eight offices and over 700 employees.

Meridith has devoted the past 23 years to community work in Arizona (including having established the Greater Phoenix Black Chamber of Commerce and the Arizona Tourism Alliance). She has a life-long commitment to minority community viability and economic development, particularly in the recreation, hospitality and tourism industries. Her 17-year-old firm provides lobbying at local and Federal level; partnership development; technical writing; conflict and crisis management; and human, cultural and natural resources development. DMCI enhances organizations' relationships with the clients, customers, employees, government and the media.

Meridith is also passing her knowledge and skills onto younger generations. She taught young executives leadership, business, and communication for Cornell University online for ten years. She is currently teaching tourism, recreation and sports marketing to undergraduates at Arizona State University.

Meridith is a well-known public figure in Arizona. She has received many awards from local governments, business organizations and non-profit group. She received the first-ever BLM Legend Award. Her government career was chronicled in the autobiography—*Thoughts While Chillin'*. Her new follow-up book *The Year a Roof Rat Ate My Dishwasher: An Arizona Survival Guide for Entrepreneurs* provides guidance to businesspeople, who are living in or thinking of relocating to Arizona, and is based on lessons from her private and non-profit experiences from 2000-2018.

Meridith is a popular speaker and can be reached at denisemeridithconsultants@cox.net about being a keynote speaker or panel member at your future conferences. Readers can sign up to receive her free blog—Thoughts While Chillin'—which has been providing weekly leadership tips for over ten years at:

https://tinyurl.com/mlvykvh

Made in the USA
Columbia, SC
17 September 2019